Contents

Preface

Macmillan Drama Anthologies

Macmillan Drama Anthologies offer a series of lively and stimulating play scripts to be read in class or presented for performance. The series is aimed at a range of age-groups, from middle school to upper secondary level, and will include scripts in a variety of genres – documentaries, musicals, and radio and TV adaptations. The plays are accompanied by source material and advice on presentation.
Follow-up ideas for improvisation, written work and discussion are included so that work on the scripts can be extended in the English or drama lesson.

Macmillan Drama
Anthologies

Taking Issue

Edited by Dan Garrett

In the Firing Line
Tony Coult

Siege at Kangaroo Hill
Tony Coult

Accident Report
Peter Spalding

What Are We Voting For?
Michael Maynard

Published by arrangement with
BBC Books, a division of BBC Enterprises Ltd.

M
MACMILLAN
EDUCATION

For permission to perform these plays, application should be made to the Permissions Department, Macmillan Education, unless no admission charge is being made.

The role-playing notes on pp. 100-108 may be photocopied for educational use.

First published 1988

Published by
MACMILLAN EDUCATION LTD
Houndmills, Basingstoke, Hampshire RG21 2XS
and London
Companies and representatives
throughout the world

Printed in Hong Kong

ISBN 0–333–46709–4

British Library Cataloguing in Publication Data
Taking Issue. — (Macmillan Drama
Anthologies).
1. Drama in English, 1945 – Anthologies
I. Garrett, Dan   II. BBC School Radio
822'.914'08
ISBN 0–333–46709–4

Introduction

The world is full of issues, and many of them concern each one of us.

Whether we know about such issues depends on whom we rely on to inform us. Many newspapers, especially the tabloids, blow up domestic tales of murder and divorce, effectively smothering the bigger issues which in the end will have a greater effect on our lives. The news on television is more responsible, but the quick cutting from one item to the next makes it hard at the end to recall what you've seen. In any case the amount devoted to each item is – in terms of what is actually put across – very brief. The views of people involved are reduced to a kind of shorthand.

At the other end of the scale, for people who are well-informed, there is what Bob Geldof calls 'compassion fatigue'. It is simply impossible for an ordinary person to get worked up about every single issue – there are just too many of them.

This volume of plays inhabits a middle ground. It takes four very different issues and approaches them in a way that tries to show the connections between ordinary people and apparently distant large-scale issues.

The plays are for a wide age-range in the secondary school. They are for English and Drama classes and for Personal and Social Education as well as for Religious Education. There are extensive suggestions at the back of the volume for follow-up work in discussion, writing and role-play. *Taking Issue* will be useful both to introduce lively dramatic literature, and to start discussion on topics which young people today find important and close to their interests.

For the increasing numbers of students taking GCSE and A-level drama, these short plays can provide ideal material for examination presentation. They will stretch young actors without being beyond their range, and because each play has several changes of location, offer an interesting challenge to the student set (or lighting) designer.

The follow-up ideas for *What Are We Voting For?* include a role-play simulation exercise about the issues involved when a town council wants to knock down a school and build a new shopping mall. Teachers of Personal and Social Education will find this of particular value in developing an understanding of how democracy operates, both within a group and at the local council level. The role-play approach gives school students plenty of opportunity to express their own views in a constructive form.

The four plays were originally commissioned for the BBC series Drama Resources, which is part of the Educational Radio output for secondary schools. Some of them may still be heard as repeats or as cassettes. They have been arranged in this anthology so that there is a progression from one play to the next – which is not to stop them being used on their own. Each play is self-contained.

In the Firing Line is – on the face of it – about two young people who get involved in a strange old lady's struggle to preserve a piece of common ground. But it raises the whole issue of why we feel strongly about our 'home territory' – and why we feel a need to defend it.

Since the Bicentenary in January 1988, Australia has been in the news in a way that hasn't happened since people rushed to become £10 emigrants in the 1950s. Siege at Kangaroo Hill looks at a very topical issue, the clash between Aboriginal land rights and the needs of Australian industry to mine ore. It's also

– strangely perhaps – a poetic piece which raises important questions about human beings and their relationship to the landscape which supports them. There are interesting parallels to be drawn with *In the Firing Line*.

Accident Report takes an apparently simple situation – the crash of a train which results, sadly, in the death of its driver – but through a series of flashbacks, shows how responsibility rests on many shoulders.

What Are We Voting For? traces the stages by which a very ordinary person – someone who might be your next-door neighbour – progresses from her strong desire to create a play-space to becoming embroiled in a struggle against a property developer. On the way, she is voted in as a councillor, and the play opens up the whole issue of the need for participation if democracy is truly to work.

In the Firing Line
by Tony Coult

The characters

Nicola
Trevor
Miss Warner
Mrs Matheson
Mitchell
Major Brookes

1 *A school playground at lunchtime. The school is on the outskirts of a small town, and surrounded by a new housing estate.*

Miss Warner: Nicola! Word with you, please!

Nicola: We're late, Miss Warner.

Miss Warner: No you're not, you've got plenty of time. Where's Trevor?

Nicola: He's lost his anorak or something.

Miss Warner: He would! Never mind, as it's the first time you've done a Community Visit by yourselves I want to be sure you're well prepared. It's Mrs Matheson you're going to see, isn't it?

Nicola: Lives up Lapping Common. Up by the Army base.

Miss Warner: That's right, I remember. Social Services say she lives on her own, and doesn't see many people. Certainly not kids from a school like this.

Nicola: Don't worry, we won't scare her, Miss. (*Calls*) Trevor! Over here!

Miss Warner: Oh no. . . . what has he done to his hair?

Nicola: He's gone and dyed it, en't he, Miss?

Miss Warner: Trevor! What's all that in aid of?

Trevor: Keep me brain warm, Miss.

Miss Warner: The colour of it! Oh, never mind. I've just been telling Nicola to be gentle with Mrs Matheson. It's the first Community Visit she's received, and we want it to go well.

Trevor: I'll keep me hat on then, all right? Blimey!

Miss Warner: How are you getting up there?

Nicola: On the bus. That's why we gotta go now.

Miss Warner: Go on then. And I want to see you both when you come back, please.

Trevor: Right y'are, Miss. See yer later!

Miss Warner: Oh dear . . . poor woman. . . . Has she any idea what's about to descend on her?

2 *Later in the afternoon, Nicola and Trevor walk through the estate to the bus-stop.*

Nicola: What did you have to do that to your hair for?

Trevor: Look me best. Why shouldn't I? I don't criticise you!

Mitchell: Oi! Trevor. Where d'you think you're going?

Nicola: Who's that?

Trevor: Oh no, it's that creep Mitchell. The one who left last year.

Nicola: What's he hanging round that underpass for?

Trevor: Don't ask me. He ain't got nothing else to do, I suppose.

Mitchell: I said where d'you think you're going with your girlfriend?

Nicola: I'm not his girlfriend.

Mitchell: You had an accident with your paintbox, Trevor?

Trevor: Mind out the way, Mitchell, we gotta catch a bus.

Mitchell: Not through this underpass you aren't.

Trevor: Who says?

Mitchell: I do. This underpass is *our* territory. You go round the top.

Trevor: Blow that. We're walkin' through it.

Mitchell: Try it, and see what happens.

Trevor: You don't own that underpass, Mitchell. We'll go through it if we want.

Mitchell: Try it, then. Go on. This is our territory.

Nicola: Don't you dare, Trev. The bus'll be there soon, and I'm not waitin' for you two little boys to have your fight. I'm going the top way. You coming or not?

Trevor: All right, all right. I just don't like him telling me where I can go, that's all. Him and his mates think they own the world.

Nicola: Well, they don't. Come on, or we'll be late.
Mitchell: See yer later, Trevor. You done the right thing, boy!

Trevor:(*To himself*)   Creep. . . . I'll get you, Mitchell!

Nicola: There's the bus! Come on, run!

3 *Later, out in the countryside. Suddenly an Army helicopter zooms low over Nicola and Trevor as they walk along a narrow lane.*

Nicola: Blimey, what were that?

Trevor: Army helicopter. We're up by the Training Ground, don't forget.

(*A burst of machine-gun fire in the distance.*)

Nicola: Sounds like war!

Trevor: They're practisin'. Da-da-da! Look out, Mitchell, I got you in me bomb-sight! Eeeoww!

Nicola: Grow up will yer! Poor old woman. She must be a wreck with all that row going on.

Trevor: This her place then?

Nicola: That's it. Lapwing Cottage, it says. I'll knock. You stay back.

(*She knocks. No answer. She knocks again.*)

Nicola: She must be deaf.

(*She knocks loudly*)

Mrs Matheson: I heard!

(*The door is opened by an old lady*)

Mrs Matheson: I en't deaf. Who the devil are you?

Nicola: Community Visit programme. Lapping Hill School.

Mrs Matheson: Oh that. I remember. You want me to help you with summat. That it?

Nicola: Well, not exactly. . . . It's more like *we've* come to help *you*. In case you wanted anything doing. Or you're lonely or anything.

Mrs Matheson: Lonely? It's like Piccadilly Circus up here. Anyway, come in, come in.

(*She closes the door*)

Mrs Matheson: Who's that then?

Nicola: Oh, that's Trevor. He's helping me.

Mrs Matheson: Trevor. Take your hat off, Trevor. 'Ten't polite indoors.

Trevor: I'll keep it on if that's all right.

Mrs Matheson: No it en't. Where's yer manners!

Trevor: All right, then.

Mrs Matheson: What the. . . .? (*She starts to giggle, then to guffaw*) What's he done. . . to his head? . . . Oh dear! Sorry, I'm sure. . . . Accident, was it? Top o' the sauce bottle come off? Eh? Oh dear, oh dear. . . .

Trevor: No! I dyed it.

Mrs Matheson: Well I tell you this, boy. You give me the first good laugh I had in months. You're welcome boy, you done me a good turn already. And what's your name, m'dear?

Nicola: Nicky.

Mrs Matheson: Nicky. You a girl?

Nicola: Yes I am!

Mrs Matheson: Blow me! Ha-ha! Daft old world, ennit? Nicky
the girl. And Trevor with the hair dyed. Up from the school
to give old Ma Matheson a helping hand. Oh dear. . . (*Her
laughing quickly turns to tears.*) There. Now look.
Blubbin' like a little child. Take no notice.

Nicola: What's up? Was it something we said?

Mrs Matheson: Course it weren't! No. No, it's that letter the
Army sent. Put me right out, that has. I tell you, gal, if I had
a gun, I'd be out there, fightin' the whole blessed Army
meself. Helicopters an' tanks an' all! I'd show 'em!

Nicola: What's this letter, Mrs Matheson?

Mrs Matheson: I'll show you. Trevor! Fetch it down, boy. On the
mantelshelf by your head. Behind the clock.

Trevor: This one, is it?

Mrs Matheson: That's him. Read it out.

Nicola: Oh, he's not very good at reading . . .

Trevor: I am. I'll read it, wait. . . . Says its from the Army at
Lapping Hill Training Camp. Says: 'Dear Mrs Matheson, As a
local resident and neighbour of the Training Camp, we would
like to inform you that the Ministry of Defence has decided to
extend the Training Camp by approximately one thousand
metres to the West. . .'

Mrs Matheson: D'you see? D'you see that? Taking my land off of
me!

Nicola: Your land? Oh, no, they're going to knock your cottage
down? Oh that's terrible!

Mrs Matheson: I'd like to see 'em try! No. They're goin' West.
T'other way from here.

Nicola: But you said 'your land'. You don't own any land, do
you, Mrs Matheson?

Mrs Matheson: Own the land, gal? No. No one does. It's
   common – always has been. Lapping Common, they call it.
   And what's more, there's the old church up there. St Jude's.
   When the old village died off, they closed it down. But that
   Church is where th' Army says it wants to go. The common
   and the church. They want it for their shootin' and
   helicopterin'. And I can't abide the thought. No, I can't!

Nicola: But. . . . if it's not used anymore . . . the church . . . and
   you're a long way away from where they want to go, I don't
   see why you're so worried.

Mrs Matheson: Listen to me, my gal. When I was a little gal, I
   used to play up on *all* that Common. All where they've got
   the Trainin' Ground now. Summertime, everyone come up
   here. Do their courtin', do their thinkin'. And us kids'd play,
   scare ourselves with gettin' lost in the woods. Blackberryin' in
   the summer, skatin' on the ice ponds when it were dark
   winter. Then the last war, and the Army come, and they put
   the barbed wire up and the Common had gone. And now they
   want more – the old church an' the graveyard. An' that's
   special to me, know why? 'Cos my old ma and pa lie up there.
   And now they wanna put young soldiers in there, wi' their
   hard boots, an' their shoutin' and shootin'.

Trevor: But it says here, in the letter. . .

Nicola: Shush!

Trevor: No, listen, it says they won't ever go inside the
   graveyard. Or the church. Just the land around it. Look, you
   read.

Mrs Matheson: Don't matter what they say. All that land belong
   to *us*. That's why they call it a *common*. They got no right to
   take it off us, no right! There now. . . . I'm sorry . . . you
   come up from the school, an' I've forgotten what for. Summat
   I gotta do for yer, wasn't it?

Nicola: It's *us* who're supposed to help *you*, Mrs Matheson. But I
   don't know what we can do.

Trevor: Could do her shopping.

Mrs Matheson: Do me own shopping, ta.

Trevor: We could dig her garden.

Mrs Matheson: Don't want no one in my garden. And why don't you speak to me, boy? I'm here, en't I?

Trevor: Sorry.

Mrs Matheson: My Jack fought the war, y'know. *And* he died in it. So don't go thinkin' I'm against the soldiers. But why do they need more land? Why?

4 *Back on the estate, Trevor and Nicola walk towards the school.*

Trevor: Well, I don't see what all the fuss is about. The Army says it won't even touch her precious church and graveyard.

Nicola: You heard what she said, it's land she knows.

Trevor: Don't mean she owns it, though. Don't mean she's gotta have a say in it.

Nicola: Why not? You think you've got a say in that underpass we've just walked through. You reckon it's as much yours as Mitchell's and his mob.

Trevor: That's different.

Nicola: No, it isn't!

Trevor: Course it is!

Mitchell: Oi!

Nicola: Oh no! Talk of the devil.

Mitchell: I thought I told you. Keep out of there!

Trevor: Shut it, Mitchell. Go and play Hard Man somewhere else.

Nicola: Trevor, don't! Just walk on.

Trevor: Why? You don't mind that old woman stickin' up for *her* place. Why shouldn't I?

Mitchell: You've had your last warning, Trevor.

Trevor: Get lost, Mitchell. You wanna fight about it, I'll give you one.

Mitchell: You wouldn't dare.

Nicola: Oh, I give up!

Trevor: Try me then. Go on.

Mitchell: Not now. I'm busy. Friday. After school.

Trevor: Friday. OK.

Mitchell: And you'd better bring a rubbish bag to put the pieces in. Cheers!

Trevor: (*To himself*) Put you in, more like, Mitchell.

5 *The classroom.*

Nicola: Trouble is, she won't let us do any gardening or shopping or anything like that. Just keeps going on about the Army and the Training Ground.

Miss Warner: Perhaps you should go up there?

Nicola: What? The Army base?

Miss Warner: To talk to them. See if they'll do anything to allay Mrs Matheson's fears.

Nicola: And do what? I don't see the point.

Miss Warner: Well, at least it'll be a chance for them to speak to her personally. It might make her feel better, even if nothing's changed.

Nicola: So what's the point – if nothing's changed?

Miss Warner: Maybe it will, who knows? But at least you'll be doing something.

6 *Lapping Common Training Camp. Mrs Matheson, Nicola and Trevor are welcomed by an officer in uniform. Behind them, soldiers drill on the parade ground.*

Major Brookes: Good morning! Mrs Matheson, isn't it? I'm Major Geoff Brookes. I'm in charge of Public Relations here at Lapping Common Training Camp. And these good people are. . .?

Mrs Matheson: They're me friends. That one's Nicky. Nicola, see, a girl. And the one with the hat on's Trevor.

Major Brookes: Welcome to the camp, then, gentleman and ladies. I've asked for some tea and biscuits to be sent in. It'll be here in a moment. OK with you?

Trevor: Yeah, I'm starving!

Nicola: Trevor. . . .

Mrs Matheson: Never mind tea and biscuits, Major. What I wanna know is: what do you want to take our land for? There's souls at rest 'neath them graves.

Major Brookes: Let me say at the beginning—

Mrs Matheson: That's common land. Always has been. You could walk it, play in it, live in it, eat off it and die in it, one time a day.

Major Brookes: Mrs Matheson, could I make it clear that—

Mrs Matheson: You make it clear then, boy. That's what we're here for.

Major Brookes: Thank you. First: about the old church and the graveyard. We did check most thoroughly with the Church authorities, and they assured us that it has been many years since the church was used. Indeed, they were happy for us to use the land there because, as you may know, the church tower is in a very dangerous condition—

Mrs Matheson: Be a sight more dangerous with all that bangin' and clatterin' going on round it.

Major Brookes: The fact is, Mrs Matheson, that if the Army
   wasn't going to use that land and it stayed public, the church
   would have to be demolished on safety grounds. So in a way,
   we're going to preserve it.

Mrs Matheson: 'Preserve it?' With soldiers running wild over it?
   Over the graves of my dear old Ma and Pa?

Major Brookes: Soldiers will be expressly forbidden to enter
   either the old church building, or the graveyard itself. You
   have our assurance on that.

Mrs Matheson: So what d'you need it for?

Major Brookes: It can be used as a landmark. Something the
   men can navigate by. Like a lighthouse.

Mrs Matheson: Lighthouse? Thought you were supposed to be
   Army, not flippin' Navy!

Major Brookes: It is important for the defence of our nation, Mrs
   Matheson, that soldiers learn how to move about the
   countryside. That is why we need the land we are now
   proposing to acquire. Land which is not much used by the
   public—

Mrs Matheson: Not bloomin' surprisin', is it, with 'elicopters
   clatterin' and guns bangin'!

Major Brookes: I'm sure that as a patriotic citizen, you see the
   need for our soldiers—

Mrs Matheson: No, I don't. When the war came, you lot come
   up here and took our land off us. Well maybe. My Jack died
   in the Army, so I know about the war. But *after* the war, you
   stopped up 'ere! That's forty years and you're still here!

Major Brookes: We must always be *prepared* for war, Mrs
   Matheson.

Mrs Matheson: You gonna do *anything* about it?

Major Brookes: I beg your pardon?

Mrs Matheson: Stop this place gettin' bigger?

Major Brookes: I will certainly convey your views to the Commanding Officer. I'm sure he will give them full consideration—

Mrs Matheson: Right! I'm off. Waste a' time you two draggin' me up here. They'll take no notice. Come on.

Nicola: Mrs Matheson, wait a bit!

Mrs Matheson: What for?

Nicola: Give him a chance to explain. Give *you* a chance to say more what you feel. . . . .

(*There is a knock on the door*)

Major Brookes: Come!

Orderly: Excuse me, sir. Tea and biscuits!

Major Brookes: Thank you, Corporal. . . .

Mrs Matheson: I come here for some common sense. If I want tea and biscuits I can get them at home! You two stoppin' here, or what?

Trevor: Can't we have the biscuits, then go?

Nicola: Trevor, you behave!

Mrs Matheson: Tea and biscuits, my life!

7 *The school playground, next day. The bell for end of school goes.*

Nicola: So then she just picks up her bag and walks out. And we're sat there looking daft!

Miss Warner: Hmm. I'm not sure I know what to suggest, Nicky.

Nicola: She's so stubborn. You can't do anything for her. I tell you, Miss, I'm starting to wish we'd never got involved in all this.

Miss Warner: Well, we can't back out now, Nicky, that would be quite wrong. Let's talk about it on Monday, all right?

Nicola: Yes, Miss Warner.

Miss Warner: Right. Have a good weekend. Oh, where's Trevor?

Nicola: Trevor? Oh, he's got an appointment about now.

Miss Warner: Appointment?

Nicola: Yeah. (*To herself*) With the doctor, I reckon. . . .

8 *The Underpass on the Estate.*

Mitchell: Come on then, Trevor, I'm waiting for you!

Trevor: Just the two of us, Mitchell. I can see your mates up the back of that underpass.

Mitchell: So what? They're just watching.

Trevor: I en't fightin' you *and* that lot.

Mitchell: Up to you. So I'm King of the Underpass, right?

Trevor: Just the two of us, it was, Mitchell! That's what we said.

Mitchell: Up to you, Trevor. If you're chicken. . . .

   (*The sudden noise of a police car siren*)

Trevor: (*To himself*) Oh no, what's goin' on. . . .?

Mitchell: Oi! What's goin' on, Trev? Did you do this?

Trevor: Nothing to do with me!

Mitchell: We'll get you for this Trevor. Come on, you lot, run! He's got the cops out!

   (*Mitchell and his friends run out of the other end of the underpass and disappear across the estate. A police car screeches to a halt, and a door opens. Nicola steps out and runs across towards Trevor.*)

Nicola: (*Breathless*) Trev! Trev! Stop where you are!

Trevor: (*To himself*) What th' ell's goin' on?!

9 *The Training Ground. An ambulance and two police cars are parked by the graveyard of the old church. There's also an Army Land-Rover, and a fire engine with a turntable ladder.*

Miss Warner: (*To Nicola and Trevor*) So just as I was setting off home, Major Brookes rang up the school and asked for you two.

Major Brookes: You're the only ones she'll talk to, I'm afraid. If any of my chaps, or the police try and talk to her, she just climbs higher up in the tower.

Nicola: But it's not safe! You said yourself the church isn't safe.

Major Brookes: It isn't. That's why we've got to persuade her to come down pretty damn' quick.

Miss Warner: Do you think you could try and talk her down? Nicky? Trev?

Nicola: We'll have to, won't we?

Trevor: Yeah! We'll do it, no problem!

Miss Warner: You must be very careful. Apparently the wooden flooring in the tower's rotten.

Trevor: Don't worry, Miss Warner. We'll fetch her down, you see.

10 *Inside the church, some moments later. There's dust everywhere. Nicola and Trevor are climbing up the stone steps of the church tower. Their voices echo.*

Nicola: Mrs Matheson? Hello?

Trevor: It's Trevor and Nicky. You all right?

Nicola: Where are you? We can't see you!

Trevor: She's not here. She's gone home, I bet.

Mrs Matheson: (*A little distant*) No I en't!

Nicola: Mrs Matheson! Where are you? You've got to come down. This church isn't safe.

Mrs Matheson: No. I'm stopping.

Nicola: Why? What are you doing?

Mrs Matheson: I'm stopping here till they agree not to take any more land off us.

Nicola: It won't work like this. You'll just hurt yourself. Please come down.

Mrs Matheson: We'll see if it won't work. I've got me thermos and sandwiches.

Trevor: What happens at night-time?

Mrs Matheson: I'll go to sleep same as you.

Trevor: And fall out the window. . .

Mrs Matheson: You go back out and tell 'em to send the newspapers up here. Go on! You come to me saying you want to help me. Well, help me now. Start by telling them bobbies to go and catch a few real criminals, and then you go home.

Trevor: You can't stop here! It en't right, Mrs Matheson, its behavin' like a stupid kid!

(*Slight pause*)

Mrs Matheson: En't you ever done summat 'cos you think it's right, Trevor? Well? Trevor, you still there? Can't see yer!

Nicola: We're worried it's not safe, Mrs Matheson.

Mrs Matheson: Then tell 'em to be quick about it. They're watching me, I can see 'em from here. The police. That Major Brookes. I can see 'em, watchin' me with their binoculars. Know what else I can see from up here? The whole of Lapping Common. All them bushes and paths and trees I used to walk in when I were a kid.

Trevor: They've all gone now, Mrs Matheson. You gotta see things right.

Mrs Matheson: This old church en't gone! I can keep hold o' this.

(*Suddenly, bits of plaster and stone fall down around Nicola and Trevor. The dust makes them cough.*)

Trevor: It's fallin' to bits! It's an old ruin!

Mrs Matheson: No it en't, Trevor. It's a principle! It en't just the Army taking the land, is it? You *used* to know who the fields belonged to. *Used* to know the farmers' names. Now – it could be anybody. And tell them two police coming up the path to stay away.

Nicola: What?

Mrs Matheson: Them two. Coming to arrest me, so they reckon? We'll see.

(*She grunts with effort*)

Mrs Matheson: See this rope? Listen!

(*Another grunt. Mrs Matheson tugs at one of the bell-ropes, and a church bell chimes.*)

Mrs Matheson: If they come in, I'll ring it. Then the whole world'll know.

(*More debris falls around Trevor and Nicola*)

Nicola: Stoppit, Mrs Matheson! You'll have the whole place down.

Mrs Matheson: You keep them two away, or I'll keep ringin' the bell.

(*She grunts and heaves at the bell-rope. The bell sounds out across the Training Ground.*)

Nicola: I'll go down. Keep her talking, Trev.

Trevor: Please, Mrs Matheson, it don't matter!

Mrs Matheson: My land, Trevor! That matters! Used to hear these bells when I was a gal. Walking up. . . . on . . . Lapping Common.

(*Suddenly there's a great crack as the beam Mrs Matheson is on breaks. There's a great crash of falling stone, wood, and one of the bells crashes down. Dust flies everywhere.*)

11 *About an hour later, an ambulance sounds its siren and drives off at high speed.*

Major Brookes: He'll be all right. Just a cut on his head, they say.

Nicola: What about Mrs Matheson?

Major Brookes: She seems all right. She's gone in the ambulance with him.

Nicola: I thought the whole tower were comin' down wi' them inside it!

Miss Warner: Come on, Nicky. We'll go and visit them in hospital.

Nicola: Are you sure she's all right, Miss?

Miss Warner: Well, the last I saw of her, she was sitting by Trevor in the ambulance and they were both laughing. She kept saying something about 'an underpass'. What was all that about?

Siege
at Kangaroo Hill
by Tony Coult

The Characters
Joe Perry
Vanessa
Michael
Tommy Winmati
Harry Best
Mrs Darby
Passer-by
Aboriginal voices ('Tommy's voices')

1 *A hot summer day in the Northern Territory of Australia. The land is flat, except for some outcrops of rock, and there are few trees. A pick-up truck drives along a rough road, sending up clouds of dust. In the cab are two young people, and a driver in his forties.*

Perry: My name's Joe Perry. I'm the Community Adviser for this part of the Northern Territory in Australia. That means my job is to help sort out any problems that crop up between the Aboriginal people and the white folks who live here. The Aborigines, of course, they're the *real* Australians – lived here for hundreds of thousands of years. The whites – like me – well, we've only been here a couple of hundred years at most. Anyway, couple of weeks ago, an English mate of mine rang up and said he was over here with his kids, and would I show 'em round while he did his business for the Mining Company. Sure, I said. The Northern Territory's a beautiful place. I'd be glad to. Course, when I picked 'em up from the airport, I never guessed what they'd both get caught up in, out here in the Outback. . . . So how long are you two kids here in Oz for, Vanessa?

Vanessa: Two months. While Dad checks up on the mining.

Michael: They're going to start work round here, Mr Perry. Dad's got to report back to London how it's going.

Perry: Yeah, he told me. They reckon there's a lot of bauxite here.

Michael: Hey! Look at those rocks! All those weird shapes. Can we stop, Mr Perry, I want to go and take some photographs.

Vanessa: He's mad on his photography, Mr Perry. He never stops.

Perry: You can't go up there, Mike. Not on those rocks.

Michael: It's all right, I promise I won't be long.

Perry: Not the point, mate. That's a sacred site. It's called Rainbow Rock and we'd have to get special permission from the Aboriginal Council to go up there.

Vanessa: Surely *you* don't have to get permission, Mr Perry?

Perry: Oh yes I do, Vanessa. The Australian Government has agreed that the Aborigine people should have back some of the land the whites took off them when we first came here. It's their land now. And places like Rainbow Rock are special. They're magic places to the Aborigine People, and if we went climbing all over them, they wouldn't be magic any more. Sorry!

Vanessa: Look! What's that lying in the road?

Perry: Where? Oh yeah. . . . Looks like he's. . . . Let's hope he's just fainted!

(The truck speeds towards a man lying in the track. He is talking to himself.)

Tommy: NNN. . . Voices. . . . Voices in my head. . . why can't they leave me alone?

Tommy's Voices:

1. We are your ancestors, Tommy. You have betrayed us.

2. You have sold us to the white miners, Tommy. You have betrayed us.

3. You will never return to your tribe again, Tommy. You will die here in the hot desert.

Tommy: No, no. . . voices. . . please. . . stop. . . .

(The truck slows and stops. Mr Perry gets out and runs to Tommy.)

Tommy: Who's this? Ghosts? White ghosts?

Perry: Gives us a hand, you two! Let's get this old feller into the shade. Bring the water-bottle!

2 *(Some time later, Tommy is lying under the tree, with the water-bottle in his hand.)*

Perry: Drink a bit more water, mate. There. Feeling better?

Tommy: Thanks, Mr Perry. Better.

Michael: Is he an Aborigine, Van?

Vanessa: I think so, yes. Oh, Mike, don't take pictures!

(But Michael takes a picture)

Perry: Good thing we came along. You'd have fried out there on the road, Tommy.

Tommy: Wouldn't have mattered. . . .

Perry: Where are you going? Rainbow Rock?

Tommy: Anywhere, Mr Perry. My people are after me. I've betrayed them, and they're after me.

Perry: Betrayed them? How do you mean, Tommy?

Tommy: Who're those two with yer, Mr Perry?

Perry: Oh. . . this is Vanessa and Mike. Couple of English kids come to see Australia. Don't you worry about them. What's all this about?

Tommy: I've done a terrible thing, Mr Perry. I've betrayed my clan and all my ancestors.

Perry: You? You're the last person to do that, mate.

Tommy: It's true. Leave me here. It's best.

Perry: Not likely. Look, would you kids go and sit in the truck. I'll be along in a minute. I want to talk to Tommy.

Tommy: No! Let 'em stay. They're young. They can hear what I've done.

Perry: You sure? I want you to speak your mind.

Tommy: Tommy Winmati always speaks his mind! It's the white man who wraps his words in bundles of paper and turns the truth into lies. Let these white ones hear my story. They must hear, so that they do not betray their clan, and their ancestors. I'm dry. . . give me some water.

(*He drinks*)

Tommy: You! Boy. You know what bauxite is?

Michael: Bauxite? Well, er. . . .

Vanessa: It's the ore they make aluminium from, isn't it? It's in the rocks.

Tommy: You're right, girl. And the mining company have engines that rip open the rocks to get the bauxite out.

Michael: Mining company? Oh, our Dad works for that—

Perry: Mike, shut up, will yer?

Tommy: And these monsters that eat up the land are the reason I do not deserve to live.

Perry: Hold on there, Tommy. Weren't *you* the fellah that was talking to the mining company about them working on your land?

Tommy: My people gave me that trust, yes. I was to speak for them. But I didn't speak loud enough. I let my ancestors down, and I deserve to die.

(*Tommy is close to tears*)

Vanessa: What does he mean, Mr Perry? 'Let his ancestors down'? His mother and father?

Perry: More than that, Vanessa. See, to an Aborigine, every member of his clan that's ever lived is still . . . well, around. Like ghosts in a way. And these ghosts live around certain places. Like that rock over there Mike wanted to climb on. They're holy places.

Tommy: They are the places where the spirits live who made this

land. Long before men and women existed. In the
Dreamtime. . . .

Michael: What's he talking about? Dreamtime?

Perry: Dreamtime was when the spirits made the Earth. Made
Australia, and everything in it. That right, Tom?

Tommy: And now the white miners want to destroy a holy place.
And I have helped them do it.

Perry: What place is this, mate?

Tommy: Kangaroo Hill.

Perry: Oh. The burial ground.

Tommy: Yes. Where my ancestors are buried. Where the Great
Kangaroo is, who made my clan and the land we live on. I
have let them destroy all this.

Perry: So what happened? Why did you agree to the mining
company doing this?

Tommy: Two days ago, Mr Perry, two days ago, I drove into the
town to meet the man from the Mining Company, Mr Best.

Michael: Mr Best? Our Dad knows him—

Vanessa: Ssh!

Tommy: I'd spent weeks travelling round different families of my
clan. Some said, 'OK, you let them mine at Kangaroo Hill,
that's fine, but make sure they pay us for coming on to our
land.' Mainly the young ones, or the ones who'd been to the
cities, and become like white fellers, said that. But mostly, my
people said, 'Kangaroo Hill is holy. The spirits of our
ancestors are everywhere in that hill. Don't let the white man
tear at the land with their engines and destroy it.' So when I
went to meet Mr Best, I knew what I should do. . . .

3 *Flashback to the offices of the mining company in a nearby town.
There's a map of the Northern Territory on the wall, with*

different-coloured flags and pins stuck into it. Tommy is wearing
a suit, but Mr Best and Mrs Darby are in shirtsleeves.

Mr Best: Mr Winmati? Hi, come in. Sit yourself down. I'm Harry
Best, of the Southern Star International Mining Corporation.
And this is Mrs Darby, who represents the Northern Territory
administration.

Tommy: Hello. I'm Tommy Winmati. Didn't realise there'd be
an official person along.

Mrs Darby: Please don't think of me as 'official', Mr Winmati.
I'm here to see fair play between you and your people on the
one hand, and the mining company on the other. I'm just a
kind of referee.

Tommy: OK, fine. Sounds good to me!

Mrs Darby: Good, then let's start, shall we?

Tommy: Sure. I want to say first about Kang—

Mrs Darby: I think, Mr Winmati, we *ought* to hear from Mr Best
first. Do you mind? It's just that he's got to get to another
meeting.

Mr Best: Thanks, Mrs Darby. OK, Tommy, not to beat about
the bush. Southern Star wants to mine on your land, and
we're prepared to pay a good deal for the privilege. My firm's
always been a good friend to the Aborigine nation, as I think
you'll agree when you clap eyes on our very, very generous
offer. We're not one of those big brother organisations that
just comes on to Aborigine Land, rips it to shreds, and then
shoves off with the dollars. You fellers have been here
thousands of years. And us? At most two hundred or so.
We'll respect that, Tommy. And we'll give you a share in our
success.

Tommy: Mr Best, this is great. But there's some places we can't
let you mine. Places like—

Mr Best: OK. Details in a minute. Here's our offer. One: a
percentage cut of all the money we make on bauxite mining.

Two: on top of that, because we want to be good neighbours with you people, we're offering a grant. Call it a 'Good Neighbour' grant if you like. This is a good deal we're offering, Tommy, and no mistake.

Tommy: I agree, Mr Best. Great offer. But we must be good neighbours with the land, and with the spirits who made it. That's why we must talk about the places you can't go into.

Mr Best: Don't start making petty objections, Tommy. This offer's too good to turn down.

Tommy: I'll look at your offer, fine, Mr Best. But you must understand. The land's not mine to sign away.

Mr Best: Sure. I understand. Its your people's land. But it's Australian land, too, remember. I mean, we're all Australians, right?

Tommy: It's not that we *own* the land, Mr Best, its more like the land owns us.

Mr Best: Come again? Sorry, mate, I don't follow.

Mrs Darby: Can I try and explain to Mr Best, Tommy? Aborigine people feel that the land they live in has been entrusted to them to look after. By the spirits who made the land. And all the animals and plants and people on it. They don't own it, but they're given the land to care for. And if they don't care for it, well, that's *very* serious.

Mr Best: We don't want to take it away from them, Mrs Darby. Just dig in it for a while.

Tommy: The land is our mother, Mr Best. It gave birth to us. That is why you cannot just go tearing into it. We can't say 'OK, mining company, you come and hurt our mother.'

Mr Best: OK, OK, but you people have made agreements before for us to mine on your land. What's the problem now?

Tommy: We can do a deal on some places. But not Kangaroo Hill.

Mr Best: Oh come on, Tommy, that's the richest site of all. There's tons of bauxite there, and its almost sitting up and begging to be dug out!

Tommy: The Spirit who created my clan lives there. If you dug there, it would die, and so would my clan.

Mr Best: But it's just an ugly rock sticking up out of the bush. You people hardly ever go there.

Tommy: And you people hardly ever go into your churches. But still you treat them with respect.

Mr Best: They're buildings. Of course we respect them – they're pretty!

Tommy: And the land is *our* building. It has a beautiful roof and walls made of blue and black light. It has a floor covered in beautiful stones. Mrs Darby, I think this is a waste of time talking.

Mr Best: It's ridiculous, it's like talking to children!

Tommy: Children! *You* are the children! Breaking, destroying, you only see till the next five minutes! Break, smash, tear up the earth! No good to me, Mister mining fellah! I'm going!

Mrs Darby: Wait, Tommy, please! Harry, is there any way your company would consider making an agreement for other land? *Near* Kangaroo Hill?

Mr Best: I'm sorry, Mrs Darby. It's out of the question.

Mrs Darby: Try and see it their way, Harry. We look at land like that and we think: What can we make out of it? What can we build on it, or what can we dig out from underneath it? But to the Aborigines, land's more like a person. You can't buy and sell a person. Try and understand that, Mr Best.

Mr Best: I do understand that. I also understand that these people need money to live decent lives, and that's what I'm offering. I'm offering a deal.

Tommy: And I will make a deal!

Mr Best: Kangaroo Hill?

Tommy: Never!

Mr Best: No deal then.

Mrs Darby: Gentlemen, can I suggest a short cooling-off period? Let's have a cup of coffee, shall we? Come back in quarter of an hour or so, and see if there's some other way out of this problem? Harry?

Mr Best: Sure. If you think it's worthwhile.

Tommy: She may do. I don't. OK, Mrs Darby, I agree. I'm going for a sit-down in the park, OK?

(*He leaves the office*)

4 *A park*

Tommy: So I went out into the street and sat down in the little park outside the offices. I looked up at the hot sun, and tried to guess what I should do. I closed my eyes, and I thought of my wife, my children, my mother and father, their mother and father . . . and slowly, my head seemed to fill with voices. My family, my friends, and my ancestors from the Great Dreamtime. All talking to me. All asking me, 'What are you going to do, Tommy?'

Voices:
   1. What are you going to do, Tommy?
   2. Will you let us down? Will you destroy the place you come from?
   3. Its only a lump of rock, Tommy. We need the white man's cash.
   4. We've gotta live like whites now, mate. We need proper schools and sanitation.
   5. Remember us, and the land that we have to care for, Tommy. Remember we've been here for 40 000 years by the white man's time.
   6. Remember the great Dreamtime before that, when the

spirits made all the land. Remember, the land isn't theirs, and it isn't yours. It belongs to the whole Aboriginal nation, Tommy.

7. Don't listen to the old 'uns, Tommy. How'll we ever get on in the world without a bit of cash?

8. Forget all that stuff about spirits and ancestors, mate. It's out of date, and we need a health centre, so we can be as healthy as the whitefellers.

(*The voices start to muddle themselves up in his head.*)

Voices: Remember, remember the land . . . forget all that stuff, mate, we need the cash . . . Remember the land . . . forget it . . . remember, forget, remember, forget. . .

Tommy: Stop!

Passer-by: You all right, mate?

Tommy: Hnn? Oh . . . yes . . .

Passer-by: Been dreaming, eh? Drop too much in the bar at lunchtime?

Tommy: Eh? Come here and say that! I'll teach you to insult me!

Passer-by: Keep yer hair on, chum. Blimey, only tryin' to help a fellah. If that's all the thanks you get . . .

Tommy: . . . and so I went back to the offices of the mining company. Looking through the window, I could see Mr Best at his desk. He is talking, but there is no one in the room. Who is he talking to? His ancestors, perhaps? But they must be thousands of seas and deserts away. Perhaps in that place he calls 'England'?

5 *Tommy enters the office. There is no pause in the action.*

Mr Best: . . . no, just making a call to Head Office, mate. Using the old satellite, you know? Bleep bleep, up in the sky? Marvellous little thing, don't yer think? Magic! Magic!

Mrs Darby: Sorry to keep you waiting, gentlemen. Now, let's see if we can get something sorted out here, shall we? Mr Best has something he wants to say, I believe.

Mr Best: Yeah. The fact is, I've been speaking to London about this problem, and they want a decision pretty smartish.

Tommy: Why must we hurry? There is time to talk.

Mr Best: London says this thing's been in the air for two-and-a-half years now.

Tommy: Two-and-a-half-years? Kangaroo Hill's been there for millions of years. And the Spirits who made it were there before Time even started. Now you want to get your hands on it in one afternoon!

Mr Best: Tell him what the Government says, will you, Mrs Darby?

Tommy: What is this? What government?

Mr Best: I'm afraid it's bad news, Tommy. I've been through to the Government Office, and they say they will allow mining to go ahead there.

Tommy: They can't. We haven't agreed!

Mrs Darby: I'm afraid the law of Australia says they can, Tommy. If they say it's in the interests of all Australians, they can override your wishes.

Mr Best: So let's deal, eh Tommy?

Tommy: Liars! You whites are liars! You ask me to talk with you, but for no reason! You promise what? Money? So my people can buy your alcohol and turn themselves into animals without spirits. You are going to violate our holy places, and you offer us money to shut up. You are liars!

Mrs Darby: Be fair, Tommy. How that money is spent is up to you and your people. You could build a hospital, or a school, or buy vehicles for the ones who want to set up as farmers.

Tommy: Liars! All of you!

Mrs Darby: You ought to try and see the good side of Mr Best's offer. It's a very good deal he's offering you, a very good deal indeed . . .

Tommy's Voices:
1. We need that school, Tommy, do a deal with them . . .
2. Remember the land, Tommy, remember your ancestors . . .
3. We're living in the 1980s, mate. We need money more than we need a lump of rock with a few old bones in it . . .
4. Remember what the whitefellers did to us, Tommy. They killed the Aborigine man when they came here. They murdered and killed and took our land from us . . .
5. It's our land, Tommy. If we want to let the whitefellers mine it, we will!
6. Respect, Tommy, respect the land . . . it's where you'll go when you die and come to us . . .
7. Do a deal, mate. Do a deal.
8. Destroy the land and you destroy the nation . . .
9. Do a deal, mate, do a deal . . .

Mrs Darby: . . . Mr Best's offer – it's a very good deal he's offering you, a very good deal indeed. Tommy? Are you listening to what I'm saying?

Tommy: I need to talk . . . I need to talk to my people . . .

Mr Best: You've been doing that for two-and-a-half flaming years! You're the one who speaks for them. *You* decide!

Tommy: There's nothing to decide, is there? If I agree to your deal, you will destroy the sacred burial ground at Kangaroo Hill, but you will pay my people. If I don't agree, you will still destroy it, but we get nothing. Right? Is that right, Mr Best?

6 *Back in the present, in the Outback.*

Michael: What happened then, Mr Winmati? Did you take the money?

Tommy: What do you think, boy?

Vanessa: You didn't have any choice, Mr Winmati. The laws of Australia said they could go ahead and dig. There was nothing you could do.

Tommy: It's my name that's on those white bits of paper. I gave in.

Michael: But will you get the money all right? The Good Neighbour grant, and the share of the profits?

Tommy: Oh yes. I think so. Small share of 'em. And a few jobs maybe. Some of us'll do all right. For a few years.

Perry: Tommy, let me help. I'll go to your clan and explain. I'll tell them you had no choice.

Tommy: They know that. But they have to punish me. They're singing me up now.

Vanessa: 'Singing him up'? What's that, Mr Perry?

Perry: It's a kind of curse. A punishment for doing wrong.

Tommy: So leave me now, please. Leave me.

Vanessa: We can't! It's not fair!

Michael: We'll ask my father to do something. He works for the mining company.

Perry: All right, Michael, that'll do. Let's go.

Vanessa: But what about Tommy?

Perry: Come on, back to the truck.

Vanessa: We can't leave him!

Perry: Do as I say. We'll talk in the truck . . .

7 *In the truck. Vanessa won't let the matter drop.*

Perry: . . . I *know* it's not fair, Vanessa, but it's their way.

Vanessa: You can't let him stay there and die!

Michael: Why don't we call the police?

Perry: And cause a riot? You've got to respect people's way of doing things. I know it's hard . . .

Michael: I can still see him. Look. Under that tree. Why must they kill him? It's only a lump of rock. He was only doing his best . . . it's not fair.

8 *Mr Best's office at the Southern Star International Mining Corporation.*

Michael: . . . it's not fair, Mr Best!

Mr Best: Hey, hold on! I know *you* must be Michael, because your father asked me to have a word with you. But who's this—?

Vanessa: I'm Vanessa. I'm Michael's sister. We wanted to talk to you about Mr Winmati.

Mr Best: Tommy Winmati? You friends of his?

Michael: We found him lying in the road yesterday. Mr Perry did. He was ill—

Vanessa: Not Mr Perry. The old man.

Michael: Lying in the road, and he thinks he's going to die—

Mr Best: Hold on! What? Die?

Vanessa: Because you made him sign the agreement about Kangaroo Hill.

Mr Best: Now wait a minute—

Michael: His clan have thrown him out. They're going to sing him up. That means he'll die. You must do something about it.

Mr Best: He signed that agreement freely. He didn't have to. He could have stuck by his principles and not signed.

Vanessa: Yes, but . . . he thought he was doing the right thing at the time. When he got back to his people and told them what he'd agreed to, then he realised it was wrong.

Michael: And now he's dying. And it's not right. You could save him.

Mr Best: Look, kids. I understand your concern for old Tommy Winmati. I like the bloke, I respect him. He's fought hard for his people's rights and I'm sorry to hear he's ill. But I've got to fight hard for my company. They're the ones who pay my salary. We both signed that agreement, in front of a neutral witness. And he got a damn' good deal. There's a lot of his folks will be grateful to him.

Vanessa: But the ones that don't want the new ways, *they're* not grateful. They think he's betrayed them. And Tommy agrees with them. He hates himself for doing it.

Mr Best: Then you should speak to those old guys who are putting this curse on him. Not me. I'm a mining engineer, darling, not a witch-doctor.

Vanessa: But it's *your* mine. Why do you need more land? Why couldn't you manage without Kangaroo Hill?

Mr Best: Let me ask you a question. You come from England, right? How did you get here?

Vanessa: From England? We flew.

Mr Best: You flew. Did you grow wings? No. You took the jumbo-jet. Which is made of aluminium, mostly, which is made of bauxite, mostly. You had a can of coke today, Mike?

Michael: I might have done, yes.

Mr Best: That can – made of aluminium, which comes from bauxite. Now then, without mines like Kangaroo Hill, no planes, no coke-cans.

Vanessa: But couldn't you get the bauxite from somewhere else?

Mr Best: Another Kangaroo Hill? And there'll be other guys like Tommy objecting. The fact is, Vanessa, that it's mining that keeps us prosperous here in Australia, and don't forget that these Aborigines are Australians too. They'll get the benefits as well.

Vanessa: But it's their land. It's their home. You came along and took it from them.

Mr Best: Not me. Maybe some long-lost ancestor of mine did, a couple of hundred years back. But *I* certainly didn't.

Vanessa: But they think their ancestors live where they were buried. Like ghosts.

Mr Best: Ancestors? Look, that's superstition. When did *you* last think about *your* ancestors? Past your granny, anyway. It's *land* we're talking about. Australian land. And it's up to all Australians to choose what to do with it.

Vanessa: But . . . Mr Best, he'll die if we don't do something!

Mr Best: Then there's absolutely nothing you or I can do about it, Vanessa. Absolutely nothing at all! Excuse me, I have other business to deal with.

(*Mr Best leaves the office.*)

Vanessa: Come on, Michael. Let's go and sit in the park. I'm going to cry in a minute.

Michael: Why won't he listen to us, Vanessa? He knows Dad, doesn't he?

Vanessa: I think Dad might agree with him. He'd say its none of our business.

9 *They go into the park outside the offices.*

Perry: Hey! Vanessa! Mike!

Michael: It's Mr Perry.

Perry: There you are. Thought I'd lost you. I've just come from Rainbow Rock.

Vanessa: Where Tommy was?

Perry: Right.

Michael: Is he . . .? Has he died?

Perry: No. Well at least, I don't think so. He's not there. And I've checked with his people. He's not there either.

Vanessa: Where do you think he is, Mr Perry?

Perry: I don't know. What I hope is that he's been taken in by someone and looked after. Maybe another clan. Or a missionary perhaps. But for now, you'll have to stop worrying about him. We've got to get you on that plane to Canberra tomorrow. And you've got packing to do.

Vanessa: We can't just leave without knowing what happened to him. It wouldn't be right.

Perry: If I get any news I'll let you know. Now, into the truck, please, or we'll be late for supper.

Michael: But Mr Perry . . .

Perry: In! I promised you. I'll let you know.

The next day, I took Michael and Vanessa to the airport. I tried to cheer them up a bit by telling them they'd be flying over Kangaroo Rock on their way to Canberra. But I'm not sure it did much good. Anyhow, on the road back, I switched the truck radio on.

Radio Announcer: Goo' day, this is Radio Station NT5, based in Darwin, Northern Territory. And top of the news this morning we have a report from Kangaroo Hill, the Aboriginal sacred burial site, where mining operations by Southern Star Mining have been halted since this morning by a man who has shut himself up in the explosives shed and is threatening to blow himself up. The man is thought to be thirty-year old Thomas Winmati, and it is thought he is protesting about the mining company's operations on Kangaroo Hill. Police and emergency services are at the scene, and efforts are being made to speak to the man. Over now for a live report from Kangaroo Hill . . .

Accident Report
by Peter Spalding

The characters
The Coroner
Driver Edward Lowe
Guard Sid Parker
Don Bellamy
Mrs Clarke
Mrs Donaldson
1st Girl
2nd Girl
Greeney
Nobbo
Hargreaves
Lester, a solicitor
Sue Morris
Michael Morris, her brother
Tony Watson
Voices (females and males)

Accident Report

by Peter Spalding

A Coroner's Court. The Coroner is sitting at a table and there is a witness box. A separate space contains the railway carriage and other locations.

Coroner: Ladies and gentlemen, this Coroner's Court is assembled to conduct an inquest into the death of a railway driver, Mr Edward Lowe, on Saturday, 14 December. He was in charge of a two-coach paytrain running between Camford and Norton when he was killed in an incident near a level crossing. We are here to decide the cause of the driver's death and to decide who – if anyone – was responsible for the accident. Our first witness, Mr Donald Bellamy, was a passenger on the train. He heard the guard and driver talking on the platform and through his eyes we can hope to get a general idea of the opening stages of the train's journey.

(We hear the sounds of a railway station with trolleys, etc, conversation in the distance and a DMU (diesel train) ticking over. Faint at the moment but approaching all the time, the sound of football supporters chanting. Across this is a Tannoy announcement)

Tannoy: The 20.52 paytrain to Cattleford and Norton now standing at platform 4 is calling at Cressington, Downing, Cattleford and Norton. Passengers for London change at Norton.

(The chanting sounds a little nearer)

Driver: We've got customers again, Sid.

Guard: They're no trouble. Their lot won today, anyway.

Driver: Then they'll be all excited—

Guard: It's not them. It's keeping the other passengers away from them – that's my trouble!

Driver: Rather you than me. I'd blow my top with the little—

Guard: *(Chuckling)* Oh I don't know. It's a bit like running a Sunday school outing really.

(*They laugh*)

Driver: What do you make it, Sid?

Guard: Fifty-one coming up.

(*The Tannoy announcement is heard behind the following dialogue*)

Tannoy: The 20.52 to Cattleford and Norton is now leaving from platform 4. Change at Norton for London.

Driver: I'll get aboard, then.

Guard: Righto.

(*Diesel motor revs, stationary*)

Mr Bellamy: Hello, Sid!

Guard: Hello, Don! Everything all right?

Bellamy: Not bad. What was it like coming in?

Guard: Bit misty.

Bellamy: Forecast is fog.

(*He gets into the carriage*)

Guard: That's all we want. Specially if that lot are getting on.

Bellamy: You can handle them.

(*Two elderly women approach*)

Mrs Clarke: (*Calling from the distance*) Is this the Norton train?

Guard: Yes ma'am.

Mrs Donaldson: Of course it is, Dora. Don't you recognise the guard? Good evening!

Guard: Good evening, Mrs Donaldson!

(*Football chant now quite close. Mrs Clarke and Mrs Donaldson get into the carriage. Mrs Donaldson looks out of the window*)

Mrs Donaldson: Er . . .?

Guard: Yes ma'am?

Mrs Donaldson: Do you think that lot are coming on your train?

Guard: Afraid so. But don't worry, I'll—

Mrs Clarke: I suppose you couldn't just blow your whistle now and get away before— ?

Guard: Sorry. It's not quite time.

Mrs Donaldson: I complained to your mate a fortnight ago—

Mrs Clarke: But he said he couldn't do anything.

Mrs Donaldson: I hope you can do something. (*Lowering her voice as if mentioning something obscene*) They're football hooligans aren't they?

Guard: Well – not really – just excited and a bit cheeky but not—

Mrs Donaldson: Well! I don't know what this country's coming to!

Bellamy: You can say that again!

   (*He retires behind his newspaper*)

Guard: Come on, you lot. Are you coming or not?

   (*The chanting has stopped*)

1st Girl: Where's Nobbo?

2nd Girl: You know!

   (*They both giggle*)

Greeney: (*Shouting very loudly*) Nobbo! . . . Nobbo!

Guard: Oi! Are you coming, or—

1st Girl: Sorry! We're waiting for somebody.

Guard: The train's going now, miss.

Greeney: 'ang on, will yer? (*Shouting*) Nobbo! . . .

Ragged chorus: (*All shouting*) Nobbo! Train's going! Nobbo! Come on!

Greeney: (*At a slight distance*) Oh, let's leave 'im! Get in 'ere!

(*They get in further down the train*)

Mrs Donaldson: Thank heaven for that! We shan't have their company in here!

(*Chorus from outside*)

Voices: There's Nobbo! Come on Nobbo!

(*Nobbo runs fast. The Guard blows his whistle.*)

1st Girl: (*Opening carriage door*) Come *on* Nobbo!

(*Nobbo gets nearer. Train motor revs.*)

2nd Girl: Oh, it's starting! Get in here Nobbo. Quick!

(*Train begins to move as Nobbo is dragged aboard and the door is slammed behind him.*)

Mrs Donaldson: (*Disgusted*) Well, really!

1st Girl: (*Admiringly*) You are a nurk, Nobbo! Why didn't you—

Nobbo: (*Approaching*) There's room 'ere . . . !

Mrs Donaldson: There's no room on this seat.

Nobbo: Plenty of room.

Mrs Donaldson: It's a non-smoking department.

Nobbo: That don't matter. (*Addressing the girls*) Where's the others? (*Shouting along the gangway*) Greeney! . . . Greeney!

Mrs Donaldson: Oh dear! I can't stand this.

Nobbo: Bring your lot up 'ere.

(*Greeney and the rest of the fans are heard approaching noisily along the gangways*)

Mrs Clarke: If they are going to stay here, shall we move down the train?

Mrs Donaldson: Certainly not. Anyway, it's smoking down there.

Mrs Clarke: What shall we do, then?

Mrs Donaldson: I don't know! Perhaps we could get out at Cressington and phone for a taxi.

Mrs Clarke: We won't get one in this fog and it would cost the earth.

Mrs Donaldson: I'll write to the railway and claim.

(*By now all the fans are together and fill the compartment around the four older people*)

Nobbo: Who's got the bag?

(*Laughter. They open cans and packets of crisps*)

Mrs Donaldson: Now look what they're doing.

Mrs Clarke: Tut, tut!

Mr Bellamy: I expect the guard'll be along to keep an eye on them. If not, I know one or two of them – and their families.

Mrs Clarke: Oh, would you?

Mr Bellamy: Yes. Don't worry.

(*The fans start the football chant, which builds up threateningly and then cuts abruptly*)

Coroner: Now, ladies and gentlemen of the jury, while it is true that this accident might not have occurred if those young people in the train had thought for a moment about the impression they were making on some of the older people—

1st Girl: (*Calling out*) OK, so we went too far, but how were we to know that she was that sort of – well – nutter?

Coroner: I beg your pardon?

1st Girl: All right. We were wrong – right? But how were we to know that she had this idea in her head that we were some sort of drunken raving lunatics? I suppose she thought we were all going to get out flick knives, and start—

Coroner: Thank you, that will do. There was obviously a complete misunderstanding between the older people and the young football fans. I must ask you to consider what may have been going on in Mrs Donaldson's mind at this moment. From her point of view, she and the three other elderly people are surrounded and outnumbered by young people they would call hooligans.

(*Pause*)

But perhaps the accident was caused by a technical failure. We will now listen to the engineer in charge of this section of the line.

Hargreaves: If I can summarise the reports of the inspecting engineers in non-technical language, what we are saying is that we could find no obvious fault in the mechanisms of the signalling, the level crossing or the track, although the actual rails seem to be due for renewal.

(*Some murmuring in the Court as the listeners begin to realise the implications*)

Hargreaves: The damage to the driver's cab . . .

(*The murmuring stops. Attentive silence*)

Hargreaves: . . . was caused by the derailment and not by impact with the car. . . . And I find myself in agreement with my very experienced colleagues when they say that it is unlikely that any fault could have suddenly developed to put the train out of the control of driver Lowe.

(*The murmur rises again*)

Coroner: Thank you, Mr Hargreaves. Are there any questions?

Lester: Please. (*Announcing himself*) Lester, trade union solicitor representing the guard Mr Parker, and relatives of the driver, Mr Lowe.

Coroner: Yes, Mr Lester.

Lester: (*Coming up from papers*) Now, Mr Hargreaves, are you telling us that this accident was definitely not caused by technical failure, but by human error?

Hargreaves: I would say that was a more likely explanation.

Lester: The signs of wear on the track – could these have been an indication that the rails were becoming unsafe?

Hargreaves: No.

Lester: Is it not a fact that this particular branch line from Camford to Norton is being run down and due for closure?

Hargreaves: Yes.

Lester: And consequently becoming somewhat neglected?

Hargreaves: No. Definitely not.

Lester: What about the rolling stock? Anybody who travels on that line, particularly on the paytrain, would agree that carriages are overdue for replacement.

(*Murmers of agreement*)

Hargreaves: But safe.

Lester: They do not appear to have been safe on the night of Saturday, 14 December, do they?

Hargreaves: I regret the loss of the driver's life as much as you do. I can only say that those coaches are safe when taken along at the correct speed.

Lester: Are you saying that, at the time the train approached the level crossing at Cattleford the speed was excessive?

Hargreaves: It is all in my report and the Coroner has a copy. In it we have said that the damage indicates collision at a speed that would have been somewhat high but not excessive, had conditions been normal.

Lester: I see. And are you suggesting that the speed was such that had the signal been at red, Driver Lowe could not have stopped the train in time?

Hargreaves: That is the suggestion.

(*Murmurs in court*).

Lester: But did you find anything to suggest that the signal was other than green?

Hargreaves: No, sir.

Lester: So the question of speed does not arise?

Hargreaves: It could when conditions are not normal.

(*Slight pause*)

Lester: Thank you, Mr Hargreaves.
(*The murmurs in court become clear phrases*)

Voice 1 (Female):   . . . conditions weren't normal, were they . . .

Voice 2 (Male):   Looks like the driver's fault to me. . . .

Voice 3 (Female):   . . . letting young hooligans on the trains . . .

Voice 4 (Male):   . . . bit funny about the level crossing . . .

Voice 5 (Female):   Yes, what *was* going on there?

(*Murmurs continue behind the next dialogue, mainly as odd words*)

Coroner: Any further questions, Mr Lester?

Lester: Not at the moment.

Coroner: Has anyone else a question on the technical report before I proceed to take other evidence?

(*Murmurs as before*)

Voice 1 (Male):   Well, that's it, then. . . .

Voice 2 (Male):   Human error – what's that mean?

Voice 3 (Female):   . . . means the driver takes the blame. . . .

Voice 4 (Male): . . . dead men can't answer back. . . .

Voice 5 (Female): Not fair. . . .

Voice 6 (Male): What about them yobbos who caused the trouble?

Voice 7 (Female): What *was* going on at the level crossing?

Coroner: Order, please! Order! I can understand your strong interest in this case. Many people in this court, including myself are regular users of this paytrain. We may wish to support the crews and even oppose the closure of the line. We may hope that the accident was caused by some technical failure for which no person is to blame. Nevertheless, I have a duty to perform. I must conduct this inquest according to the law.

(*Silence*)

Now, is there anyone who wishes to ask Mr Hargreaves a question?

(*Silence*)

Thank you, Mr Hargreaves. You may go. I will now take evidence from the Guard. Now, Mr Parker, how far do you think Mr Lowe, your driver, was aware of what was happening behind him on the train?

Guard: At that time he would not have been aware how things were going. Not till—

Coroner: Did you visit him in his cab at this particular time?

Guard: Yes.

Coroner: Did he seem in good health?

Guard: Then, yes.

Coroner: About what time was this?

Guard: 21.30 exactly. I checked the time to tell him that we were about eight minutes late because of the fog.

Coroner: So you are saying that, at 21.30 Mr Lowe seemed to be in good health?

Guard: Well, yes.

Coroner: Did he speak to you?

Guard: Only briefly. I never disturb him much when he's driving through fog. It was thick from Downing right through Cressington—

Coroner: What did you say?

(Train sounds. The Guard calls from the witness box)

Guard: Everything OK, Ted?

(Answering from the train)

Driver: Bit thick. It'll clear just before Cattleford.

Guard: Yeah, usually does.

Driver: How are the customers?

Guard: Settling down, I think.

(Train sounds fade)

Guard: *(To the Court)* I really thought my troubles were over by then. I had had a word with the youngsters – so had Mr Bellamy and I thought, 'We've only the fog to worry about now'. It was just then that—

Coroner: Forgive me, Mr Parker, but I wish to make something very clear to the jury. This may be rather distressing for you, but I think you will understand that we must know not only what occurred next, but the sequence of events. Your conversation with Mr Lowe in his cab took place at 21.30 and you have told us that Mr Lowe seemed to you to be in a normal state of health and although he was having to drive through what were rather tricky fog conditions, he was not showing any special strain?

(A pause)

Guard: No, not then.

Coroner: Not then. Later perhaps?

(*Another slight pause*)

Guard: Well – perhaps. After—

Coroner: Mr Parker. Tell us what happened—

Guard: What happened next was downright ridiculous or would have been but for what it led to—

Coroner: Let us have the facts, Mr Parker.

Guard: Actually, I wasn't there when she did it.

(*Train sounds. The guard walks from the witness box to the train.*)

I had walked down the train to the brake van and everything seemed to be all right.

Mrs Clarke: Well, I was dozing off when Mrs Donaldson started sniffing next to me.

Coroner: Sniffing?

Mrs Clarke: She nudged me and she said—

Mrs Donaldson: Somebody is smoking. One of those hooligans is smoking. They're doing it on purpose. (*Raising her voice and speaking loud and clear*) This is a non-smoking compartment. If this goes on I shall call the guard.

(*Greeney blows a raspberry. There is laughter, not exclusively from the young people. A number of people speak more or less simultaneously.*)

Mr Bellamy: Oi! Show a bit of respect!

1st Girl: That's not funny, Greeney.

2nd Girl: Leave it out, Greeney, can't you?

Greeney: Why? What's wrong?

Nobbo: Leave it out!

(*Other passengers are heard asking questions and commenting, but not distinctly. Above it all, Mrs Donaldson has become hysterical and her voice rises into a scream.*)

Mrs Donaldson: Guard! Guard! Guard! Guard!

(*The train brakes. There is a general feeling of things being jerked and loose objects falling down. The train comes to a halt.*)

Nobbo: She's pulled the 'andle!

1st Girl: Now look what you've done, Greeney, you great berk!

2nd Girl: Ooh! my dad's sure to find out about this one!

Guard: (*Approaching*) Right then, which one of you did it?

(*General hubbub cut short as gangway door shuts*)

Driver: (*Approaching, very tense and angry*) Who pulled the safety? Who pulled it?

(*A pause*)

Mrs Donaldson: (*Small voice*) I did.

Driver: Why?

(*Silence, then courtroom*)

Coroner: Why did you?

Mrs Donaldson: I really can't say. . . . I can't say!

Coroner: We've established that these young people were noisy and high spirited. . . .

Mrs Donaldson: (*Quietly vehement*) They were.

Coroner: But did any physical attack or violence take place? (*Pause*) Well, did it?

Mrs Donaldson: No, madam.

(*Train*)

Driver: Do you know why she pulled the safety, Sid?

Guard: Er – no. I was just—

Driver: What sort of guard are you, then?

(*Silence*)

Guard: Ted—

Driver: Out of my way. You do your job. I'll do mine.

(*The Guard starts to follow him, gives up, and goes back to the witness box.*)

Guard: I'll never forget the way he said it. And it was the last time we ever— (*Breaks off*).

Coroner: I respect your feelings, Mr Parker, but you realise that I must question you further. The time would have been about 21.32, perhaps?

Guard: I had to take notes for a report, because the alarm cord had been pulled, you understand. And I had noted the time as 21.33.

Coroner: At what time did you finish taking notes from the passengers?

Guard: I'd say 21.50.

Coroner: And the accident occurred at 21.55 at the Cattleford level crossing?

Guard: Yes.

Coroner: Did you think of speaking to Mr Lowe between the time you have told us about and the time the accident occurred?

Guard: I thought of it, yes, but I decided not to. I wish I had, though.

Coroner: Would you have said that the way in which Mr Lowe spoke to you and his general behaviour after the cord had

been pulled was typical of him – even allowing for the
circumstances?

Guard: Well— no.

Coroner: Thank you, Mr Parker.

(*He steps down*)

Members of the jury, there is now only one piece of evidence
to come – that of the people with the car at the level crossing,
but whatever they have to tell the court, you will need to form
an opinion about the state of mind of the driver, Mr Lowe.
He was very near retirement, had been a railway man all his
life, was rather depressed about the present state of the
railways. But there is no hard evidence to suggest that the
human error which caused the accident was necessarily his.

(*Pause. Sue Morris enters the witness box.*)

Coroner: I will now take the final piece of evidence. Miss Morris,
what was the time when you parted from your brother, Mr
Michael Morris, and your friend, Mr Tony Watson, at the
Cattleford level crossing?

Sue: About ten to ten. I never realised that a train would come.
In any case, I would never have agreed to go out with Mike if
I'd known it would be so foggy.

Coroner: I take it that your brother was in the early stages of
learning to drive?

Sue: Very early—

Tony: (*In the car*) Stalled again!

Sue: Why don't we give up and go home? I don't think Mike'll
ever learn.

Tony: Oh yes he will. He's got to. His new job depends on it.

Sue: All right, Tony, but I don't know why you let him use your
car.

Mike: Because Dad won't let me use his.

Sue: Not surprising after what you nearly did to it.

Mike: Oh, let's go home. Perhaps I'll never learn.

Tony: Oh yes you will, Mike. Now just remember what you've been told. Take your time, just start up, put it in gear and drive along the road.

(Sound of car starting, at first over-revved, but then becoming reasonably stable)

Tony: That's better, now keep it steady as it goes, now slowly round the corner. I said slowly! Foot up! up! up!

(Car sounds indicate that it is nearly out of control. Sue gives a short scream. Engine stalls.)

Sue: That's it, I'm walking.

(Sue opens the door and gets out, door shuts.)

Sue: Hey, do you know where we are?

(Level-crossing warning bell)

Sue: We're on the level-crossing! Mike! Tony! You'll have to drive it off. Quick!

Mike: *(Getting out)* Sue's right – over to you, Tony.

Tony: Have we got time?

Sue: Come on, Tony.

(Sound of train hooter in distance)

Sue: That's the train! You'll have to leave the car! Out! Get out!

(Courtroom)

Coroner: And fortunately for the three of you, at least, you got clear before the train reached the crossing. Did you realise when you abandoned the car, it was directly in the path of the oncoming train?

Sue: I don't know. It was foggy. You couldn't see a thing.

Coroner: But you heard the warning bell. Surely you noticed the flashing lights and the rails crossing the road?

(*Sue doesn't answer*)

Coroner: And that is the final evidence.
Members of the jury, it should now be possible for you to arrive at a general view of the sequence of events that led to the shocking conclusion at the Cattleford crossing. But, of course, the verdict you arrive at will depend on how you've assessed the evidence and where you've placed the blame.

The football chant
Ca . . . amford, Ca . . . amford, Ca . . . amford.
  Camford,
  Camford,
  Camford.
We're going on
We're going up
We're gonna win
the FA Cup.
  UP UP UP
We're going on
We're going through
We're going to
Division Two
  Two Two Two
(*This chant could be learned by the whole class and used as a refrain to indicate time-lapse or change of place.*)

What Are We Voting For?

by Michael Maynard

The characters

Shirley Hayes
Jim Hayes
Maureen
Mr Walker
Sandra
Bob
Sue
Terry
Mr Davies
Deborah
Mr Perkins
Doris
Don
Fred Chappell
Old Lady
Jeremy
Mrs Grant
Driver
Chairperson
Action Group Members
Site-workers
Protesters

The play starts with a dramatic effect to represent an accident. Perhaps an ambulance siren and a flashing blue light. As this fades, our attention goes to. . . .

1 *Shirley's home. Jim sits waiting. He is reading a paper, but keeps looking at his watch. Shirley enters.*

Jim: Where you been, Shirley? I've been waiting an hour for my tea.

Shirley: You can stop that kind of grumbling for a start-off. I've been at the hospital.

Jim: What?

Shirley: It's Gary. He had an accident.

Jim: What was it? How is he? Is he all right?. . .

Shirley: It's all right. He's OK now. But I must admit when he came home all covered in blood, I thought he'd had it.

Jim: What happened? He hasn't been fighting, has he? If he has, so help me, I'll make sure he never. . .

Shirley: No, it wasn't his fault. He was playing on that waste ground around the corner, and some bright spark had left a smashed bottle there. He fell over and cut himself. I've never seen so much blood. Anyway, they stitched him up, give him some blood, and they say he'll only have to stay overnight.

Jim: What was he doing on the Waste anyhow?

Shirley: They've got nowhere else to play, you know that. Either they play in the street and get run over, or they use the Waste. It's not their fault. . . .

Jim: If I found the slobs who break glass bottles all over the place, I'd string them up.

Shirley: Why do people treat a place like that as a dump?

Jim: Why? 'Cos they're slobs, that's why. Give 'em an empty space and they'll fill it with rubbish.

Shirley: P'raps that's the problem.

Jim: What, the slobs?

Shirley: No . . . Jim . . . the empty space. The fact it's empty. You know how it is, if something looks like a rubbish dump, it'll be treated like one.

Jim: Give over, Shirl. They don't think about things like that. They're just slobs.

Shirley: Listen. It's only people who live round here know that heap of waste land is a play area. We must be able to do something . . .

Jim: Yeah, put up a sign, 'Kids' Play Area. . . . Clear Off!' Lot of good that'd do.

Shirley: No, we can do more than that. We've got to.

Jim: 'Ere, I hope you're not getting one of your crazy notions, Shirley.

Shirley: (*Ignoring him*) Now we'll have to get everyone involved, the whole neighbourhood.

(*She goes off*)

Jim: (*Following her*) Shirley . . . Shirley . . .

2 *Maureen's home. Maureen opens the front door to Shirley.*

Shirley: Hello, Maureen.

Maureen: Oh hello, Shirl. Sorry I'm late. Anyone else here yet?

Shirley: Yes. Twelve have turned up. We've already started chatting. Oh, and Mr Walker's come as well.

Maureen: What, that accountant chap from number 23?

Shirley: Yes.

Maureen: Ooh, I'd have thought it'd all be a bit below him.

Shirley: No. Seems quite interested. He's useful actually, 'cos he knows all the ins and outs of things – how to organise and that. Come on through.

(*They go through to the front room where there is a buzz of conversation*)

Walker: (*Speaking above the others*) No, you see, as I was saying, it's a three-stage approach I would advocate. Firstly, we have to decide what's to be done with the site, then how to do it, and thirdly, who is to do it.

Sandra: Yes, I agree.

Shirley: Yes, well, I've been thinking about that . . .

Bob: Funny you should say that. See I remember, in 1952 it was, we tried to do something like that . . .

Sandra: Sshh. . . . Not now, Bob.

Bob: Look, I was only saying . . .

Sandra: Quiet. What were you saying, Shirley?

Shirley: Well, I was thinking about things we could do. Like, if we turned it into a really good play area. You know, like an adventure playground . . . and a garden too. We'd have to clear it all up first. Then dig over the ground. But we could have part of it as a kind of rest garden, with benches and stuff for mums with small kids. . . .

Maureen: Oooh, good idea. When I come back from the shops with my little'n, I'd love a sit down . . . just to break up the journey.

Shirley: That's what I thought. And then the rest of it could be an area for the older kids. We could build some structures, climbing things, ropes and that. Well . . . whatever the kids would like. Take some work, though.

Bob: You can say that again, I remember with the Jubilee street party. All that bunting had to be hung and . . .

Sandra: Not now, Bob. We're talking about the future, not the past.

Walker: The thing is, we'll need people to organise this. I mean we are already a sort of ad hoc action group, but I think we should constitute ourselves formally and elect a chairman.

Maureen: What do we need a chairman for?

Walker: Somebody to coordinate activity and organise things. And to act as a focal point for interested people to get in touch with.

Maureen: I see.

Sandra: Well, how do we choose somebody?

Bob: I remember in '46, just after the war, we had to elect a chairman of our tenants' association . . .

Sandra: Bob . . .

Bob: Yes?

Sandra: Shut it.

Bob: Oh.

Walker: So I suggest we nominate people we think would suit the position.

Sandra: I think you should do it, Mr Walker. You know about these things.

Walker: That's very kind of you. Obviously I would do the job to the best of my ability. (*Pause*) Well, if there's no other nominations, I suppose we'd umm. . . .

Maureen: Hang on a minute. I think Shirley'd be the best person. After all, she started all this and got the whole thing going. She should be the chairman.

Bob: Chairwoman it would be then, wouldn't it?

Maureen: Well, whatever. Would you do it, Shirl?

Shirley: 'Spose so. But it depends what other people think.

Walker: With all due respect, you must consider whether a woman is best suited to the job.

Maureen: I hope you're not suggesting our Shirley ain't any good 'cos she's a woman.

Walker: No, no, of course not. Well, if that's all the nominations, I suppose we'd better vote on it. A straight fight between the two of us. And may the best person win.

(*They shake hands*)

3 *The School Hall. A large meeting to discuss the issue. There is a general hubbubb of conversation.*

Shirley: OK, everybody. Quiet please. Right. Well, having been elected Chairperson of the Action Group, I've called this meeting 'cos I think we're ready to decide exactly what we're going to do with the space and who's going to do it. It's great to see so many youngsters here as well. After all, it's as much your space as ours, and so you ought to decide what should be put there.

Maureen: It's still a dump though, Shirley, isn't it? It'll need clearing up first.

Shirley: Right, Maureen. What I'd like at the end of the meeting, is to make a list of people prepared to put some work in. But first, what about you youngsters? Have you done what I asked you, and decided how you want to use the space? Yeah, Sue?

Sue: Yeah, well, we got together and . . . we had a bit of a row really. 'Cos Gary and John wanted a football pitch.

(*Cries of laughter and derision*)

Terry: No, a small five-a-side pitch, that's all.

Sue: . . . and some of us thought the space ought to be for the toddlers. Like a sandpit and that.

(*Mumbles of 'Good idea'*)

And we also agreed with the idea of a little garden with a couple of benches.

Terry: Yeah, but it wouldn't all fit in!

Shirley: Thanks for your ideas. In a minute everybody'll have a
chance to choose. But before we vote on things. . . . Are
there any other suggestions or comments?

Bob: I just thought I'd let you know – I've got loads of tools that
might be of use, left over from when we did our place up. In
'64 it was . . . might have been '63, no . . .

Shirley: (*Interrupting*) Great . . . great, Bob, thanks. Lots of
tools.

Mr Davies: Err, excuse me . . .

Sandra: Old Mr Davies wants to say something.

Mr Davies: It's just – I love gardening. And I haven't had a
garden now for ten years, since they rehoused me. I just
wondered if there's going to be a garden . . . if I might be
able to look after it. I'm not as young as I was, but I can still
plant things and have a bash at some weeding. And I'd love to
have an area I could plan displays . . . you know. And if some
of the young uns were interested, I could teach 'em all about it.

Shirley: Thanks, Mr Davies. I hope it works out so that can
happen. First though, we'd better make some choices. Look,
I'll write the list of suggestions we've had so far, then we can
see what people think . . . and vote.

4 *The Waste. Various people are working on the site, clearing
rubbish and organising the space.*

Bob: (*Picking up a bit of scrap metal*) Look at this. D'you think
it's a priceless antiquity?

Sandra: (*Taking it*) What, with 'sardines' written on it! (*She
throws it on the pile of rubbish*)

Bob: 'Ere, pass the spade over, will you?

Sandra: Here y'are, love.

Bob: Great. I'll just get this dug . . . then the next team can get
the path laid. Oh, hello, Shirley.

Shirley: Hello all!

Bob: Is Jim coming down today?

Shirley: Yes, later – he'll be working with the kids on building the ramps.

Sandra: 'Ere, Shirl, innit great the way the kids have mucked in on all this? I've never seen 'em so involved in anything. I was trying to get our Barry to come home for his tea the other day. I couldn't get him away. . . .

Bob: I'd have thought they'd have got bored with it by now. After all, it's taking time, isn't it?

Shirley: Well, nobody said it'd be easy. I think we've achieved a lot. . . . What's it been . . . six months now?

Sandra: Must be.

Bob: Yes, we started. . . May 7th, it was. Tell a lie, May 8th. No . . . It was a Tuesday.

Sandra: Bob . . .!

Shirley: Where's your Barry now?

Sandra: He's working with Mr Davies on preparing a rose bed. Never knew he was interested.

Shirley: Yes, it's great. Seems to have brought the whole neighbourhood together, somehow. Anyway, I'll just get the wheelbarrow, and get some of that rubbish shifted. . . .

Deborah: (*Rushing in*) Shirley! Hey, Shirley!

Shirley: What is it, Deborah? Steady now.

Deborah: There's a bloke snooping around. Says he's from the Council. Look, there he is. He asked me who was in charge. I said you. I hope that's all right. Look, he's coming over.

Perkins: Ah, good afternoon. I gather you're in charge of this little escapade.

Shirley: Well, I represent the Action Group, yes.

Perkins: I must say you've made quite a difference here. This used to be nothing but waste ground.

Shirley: You don't need to tell us that.

Perkins: Yes, a remarkable job.

Shirley: Thanks.

Perkins: Shame it's all for nothing.

Shirley: What d'you mean, nothing? Who *are* you?

Perkins: I'm terribly sorry, I quite forgot. Forgive me, I'm Mr R. Perkins from the Works Department at the Council. I'm afraid this area is now due for redevelopment and we've granted permission for some offices to be built on this site.

Shirley: What?

Perkins: Oh yes . . . as part of the overall plan of improvements within the borough. The Council has instructed a group of contractors to develop this Temporary Open Space in accordance with the redevelopment proposals passed at the last Finance and Resources Subcommittee meeting.

Shirley: Look, hang on a minute. I don't understand all this. Are you saying you're going to destroy all we've done here? Bulldoze it all and build offices?

Perkins: Afraid so.

Shirley: But we don't want offices. We want a playspace and a garden.

Perkins: Unfortunately, you're not representative of the people.

Shirley: I was elected.

Perkins: You may represent your Action Group, but not the needs of the whole community. Your councillor does that.

(*The volunteers are gathering around listening to the argument*)

Shirley: Look, the land is on our front doorsteps. It was a

dangerous rubbish dump. We changed all that. It's taken
months . . .

Perkins: The land you have chosen to, as it were, rearrange, is
not yours to tamper with. You should have got permission.
There are procedures for all this. You should have consulted
us first.

Shirley: What about you? You didn't consult us when you left it
for years. Nor when you decided to build offices.

Perkins: The information was there. If you wished to see it, all
you had to do was ask.

Shirley: Why didn't you ask us? You don't seem to care about us
– the people who actually live here. We just get in the way of
your rotten development.

Volunteers: You tell him Shirley. Right on. That's right.

Perkins: (*Snide*) Listen, you keep talking about '*we* didn't do this
and *we* didn't do that.' *We* are merely officers of the Council.
And the council is yours. Your elected representatives. If you
feel your representatives, your councillors, aren't acting on
your behalf, then there's one very simple thing you can do.

Shirley: What's that then?

Perkins: Vote them out. There's a by-election coming up. Simply
vote for somebody else who you think will represent your
interest. On the other hand, if you don't think there is
anybody, then there's a simple alternative.

Shirley: What? – me stand for election?

Volunteers: Yeah. Go on Shirl.

Perkins: Look – if you're so sure you represent the views of your
neighbours, why not?

Shirley: Maybe I will. Maybe I'll do just that. (*Half as a
joke*) You be careful. You might find me sorting your
Works Department out for you!

(*Laughter*)

Volunteers: You watch out, Matey. Shirley'll sort you out. You tell him, Shirl!

5 *A front door. Shirley knocks. Doris opens it.*

Shirley: Hello. Doris Martin, isn't it?

Doris: Yes. Hey, it's . . . Shirley isn't it? Shirley Hayes.

Shirley: Yes, that's right. I didn't think you'd remember me.

Doris: Course I do, love. Your Jim helped us with the fete that time.

Shirley: That's it.

Doris: Come in. What can I do for you?

Shirley: Well, believe it or not, I'm standing for election to be a councillor.

Doris: Councillor. . . . my word. Never thought you cared about politics.

Shirley: I didn't. I never thought it concerned me. Until this business with the playspace.

Doris: I don't know. I don't get involved in those things.

Shirley: What things?

Doris: Politics. They're all the same to me, those parties.

Shirley: Oh Doris. They're not all the same. Believe me, there's a whole lot of difference. But, well . . . politics ain't some weird foreign animal. It's all of us. . . . It's like, how we organise our lives, our neighbourhood . . . our country. Whether it's deciding to have a local swimming pool, or how many buses there are, or how much tax you pay – it's all politics.

Doris: I don't understand it, Shirley.

Shirley: Nor did I. I still don't, half of it. But I do know I was a
bit of a fool in the old days. I used to say it was nothing to do
with me. Meanwhile, other people were deciding things . . .
all about my life and that . . . and I weren't even involved.

Doris: So what do we do?

Shirley: First you try and understand what's going on. Not the
big things p'raps, but things that go on around here. . . . like
litter bins for instance; who d'you think got all those litter bins
here?

Doris: I dunno. Good job though, people were forever shoving
rubbish on me doorstep.

Shirley: It was the Action Group. Mrs Robbins came and had a
go at me about it. So we wrote to the Council and something
was done. See. . . . all politics. And with me as councillor we
could get even more things done. Improve the conditions
round here. I'm gonna fight for better housing, more places
for the kids to play. . . . repair these rotten old broken paving
stones . . . oh there's so many things. But first, I've got to be
elected. And for that to happen, I need your vote . . . and
many more like yours!

6 *A polling station on Election Day. People are wearing rosettes
and carrying banners. The banners read 'Vote for Shirley Hayes'.
The crowd chant and take up different symbolic positions.*

7 *Inside the Town Hall. Shirley is looking for the council chamber.*

Don: Hi . . . you look lost.

Shirley: Yes, I am a bit.

Don: You're Shirley Hayes, aren't you?

Shirley: Yes. . . . but. . . .

Don: It's just that I've heard a lot about you. Congratulations on
your election victory. And welcome to the council.

Shirley: Ta, but umm. . . .

8 *An echoey passage in the Council buildings.*

Don: Oh, I'm a councillor too. Don Freedman. I represent the Riverside Ward. We kept hearing reports about the new local bombshell-of-a-housewife who was stirring things up a bit.

Shirley: (*Unsure how to take this*) Oh . . . thanks.

Don: No. . . . I think it's great. Good to have you here, honest. Half of this lot just get wheeled out of old attics, still covered in cobwebs. You'll liven things up a bit.

Shirley: I hope so.

Don: You're after fighting this Development Plan, aren't you?

Shirley: You bet.

Don: Take my advice, get on the Redevelopment Working Party.

Shirley: Why?

Don: You've got to be involved where you'll have the most influence. At big council meetings, more often than not, there's so much to get through, nothing's discussed at all. In short, nobody listens. Whereas on working parties or subcommittees, you have a chance to chat. Get people to think and change their minds.

Shirley: Thanks for the advice.

Don: Mind you, that's all for the future. First of all, you'd better attend the Town Planning Meeting tomorrow night. You can see the whole thing in operation.

Shirley: Oh right. I'd better have a chat with the Action Group and prepare our case.

Don: Oh . . . and watch Fred. Councillor Fred Chappell that is, Chairman of the Committee. I warn you. He's in favour of the plan, and he holds the power.

9 *The Town Planning Meeting. The Committee members sit around chatting.*

Fred: (*No-nonsense northerner*) Right. I'd like to call the meeting to order. I'd like to welcome our three new councillors after the by-election in the Bankside Ward . . . Councillor Hayes, Councillor Tapman and Councillor Sing. Welcome. Now then, the first item concerns the Development Plan's second phase proposals. You all have a copy of the report from the Chief Officer, Works and Development Working Party. So, it there's no objections, will somebody move acceptance of these motions please? Councillor Evans, thank you. . . . right . . .

Shirley: Just a minute.

Fred: Oh . . . yes, Councillor Hayes. Your area, isn't it?

Shirley: Yes, and I strongly object to these proposals.

Fred: Oh dear. Look, I'm afraid it really is too late. You're new to all this. We've been through it before. Take my word for it. It'll be all right.

Shirley: No – no, I can't. I was elected to fight these proposals. See, that land's been left empty for years. A group of local people have got together and turned it into something.

Fred: (*Bored, and irritated*) Look, hold on a minute. Order. I appreciate what you're saying. But d'you think we're going to give up the chance of a major new development – that'll improve the whole area and bring prosperity to the whole borough? We've had all this out – last October! It's a prime site for redevelopment. An important, large, multi-national concern has declared an interest in building offices there and now you're opposing it because a few local kids haven't got anywhere to play?

(*Some grunts of, 'Exactly', 'Hear, hear.'*)

Shirley: Yes, that's exactly what I'm doing. I can see there are arguments in favour of the plans, but the Action Group that I represent . . .

Fred: Listen, Councillor Hayes. You're now a councillor. You now represent the borough as a whole, not just a handful of well-meaning activists. Go back and tell your friends that we need offices there, in the interests of the whole borough.

(*Some mumbles of agreement*)

Shirley: They're not just a handful of friends or activists, as you call them. These are local people who care about what's going on.

Fred: I dare say. All three or four of them. I know these groups.

Shirley: If you'd seen them all working on the site you wouldn't scoff like that. I demand something be done.

Fred: Too late, I'm afraid.

Shirley: I demand a public enquiry.

(*General 'Oh no's'*)

Fred: If you want to be so stupid, take it up with the Government, with the Department of the Environment. As far as this committee's concerned, this decision is not going to be stopped by a handful of troublemakers. Next item. . . .

(*Shirley protests and there is general uproar as people take sides on the issue*)

10 *The empty Committee Room. The meeting has ended. The members have left, except for Shirley who sits defeated. Don is just leaving, but comes back.*

Don: Well tried, Shirley.

Shirley: Oh, Don. It was useless, wasn't it? I didn't stand a chance.

Don: Well, he's been at it a bit longer than you.

Shirley: What can I do now? I can't go back and tell them it's hopeless. After all their effort. They've been relying on me.

Don: I didn't expect you to give up that easily.

Shirley: What can I do? He thinks I represent a few cranks.

Don: So show him otherwise.

Shirley: How?

Don: Petition. Show how much support you've really got.

Shirley: Hey, that's a good idea.

Don: And if you like, I'll arrange a private chat for you and Fred. If I've learnt one thing in my years here, it's that more is achieved over a pint in the pub than in the council chamber. Believe me.

11 *In a street. It's very cold. Shirley, Terry and Sue are talking while trying to keep warm.*

Shirley: Right then . . . come here, you two. While the others sort out the petitions, I'd just like to run through everything with you.

Terry: Shirley?

Shirley: Yes, Terry.

Terry: I don't think I understand what's going on.

Shirley: Fair enough. Look, the Council don't think I represent the views of most people. So, we're going to show them just how many people in the area object to them building offices and things.

Terry: Oh right.

Sue: Right. . . . What do we do?

Shirley: Well, you knock on the door and explain who you are and why you've called round.

Terry: Oh, do we have to?

Shirley: What?

Terry: Ain't there any other way?

Sue: What's wrong?

Terry: Nothing. I just don't like . . . oh, you know.

Shirley: You're not shy, are you, Terry?

Terry: No. It's just . . .

Sue: Look, we'll be together, won't we?

Terry: I'm no good at talking people into things. They won't listen to me.

Shirley: Course they will. I promise you. You have a go and see. I tell you, they're gonna be more nervous about it than you . . . strangers at the door and that. So take your time, say you're from the Action Group, spell everything out, and see if they'll sign. Take a few sheets . . . see how you get on. . . .

(Shirley goes off. Sue and Terry look around and then look at each other.)

Sue: Well, we'd better get on with it before we freeze to death.

Terry: Where?

Sue: *(Pointing to the nearest house)* Over there.

Terry: Why there?

Sue: We've got to start somewhere.

Terry: OK, here goes.

(They approach a front door and ring the door bell)

Old Lady: *(Calling from behind door)* Who is it?

Terry: Hello. We're two members of the Craig Road Action Group.

Old Lady: What action? Couple of muggers are you?

Sue: No. Please can we talk to you for a moment. We're asking people to sign our petition about what the Council are planning to do with our play area.

Old Lady: It's nothing to do with me. Go away.

Sue: Please open the door so we can explain. You see, it's to do with everybody. All the people in the area.

Old Lady: All right then. (*Opens door*) What is it?

Terry: We've got this petition to be presented by our councillor, Shirley Hayes, to the Council, to show how many people agree with it. I'll read it out. 'We the undersigned, strongly object to the council plans to build offices on the Craig Road site now being used as a playspace and garden. And we demand that there be a public enquiry.' Will you sign it?

Old Lady: No, I couldn't do that. I don't put my name to things. They might come round and well . . . you know . . .

Sue: No, I don't know . . .

Old Lady: They could cut my electricity or water off, couldn't they?

Terry: No, they couldn't. Lots of people are signing it. It's safe – honest.

Old Lady: Petitions won't change anything. They'll carry on and do what they want.

Terry: Not if we can show Shirley's got enough support. We can change things.

Old Lady: But I don't know anything about it.

Sue: We'll explain. If you know a bit more, maybe you'll sign.

Old Lady: No, don't bother. You seem to know what you're talking about. Give it here.

(*She takes the petition and signs it. Sue and Terry look pleased.*)

12 *A pub. Shirley is sitting at a table. Don approaches, carrying three drinks. He joins her.*

Shirley: Are you sure this is a good idea?

Don: Course I am. What've you got to lose? I told you, Fred Chappell isn't a bad bloke – he just gets cornered sometimes. Whereas in here, over a drink. . . . You'll see, he's reasonable.

Shirley: Well, if I can get through to him. . . . Oh, here he comes.

(Fred enters)

Fred: Evening, Don. Evening, Mrs Hayes.

Shirley: Shirley, please. Everyone calls me Shirley.

Don: Here y'are, Fred. I got one in for you.

Fred: Oh ta. Cheers. Well, lass, you've created a bit of a stink haven't you?

Shirley: I didn't mean to. All I've tried to do is represent the people who voted for me. That's all.

Fred: We all do that.

Shirley: I know you do . . . broadly. But, having only just been voted in, I've got a clear indication of the things my people really want.

Fred: I see that. But, this development. . . . It'll provide jobs, it'll bring the whole area prestige. People want that, surely?

Shirley: Look, it isn't going to provide jobs for people in this area. They ain't office workers. And as for prestige . . . they just want better housing, better facilities. An office block ain't gonna give 'em that.

Fred: *(Reluctant to concede)* Aye, well . . you've got a point there.

Shirley: I mean, they can't play in the streets any more. The only good place was Bensall Crescent, and that's now used as a short cut for traffic going into town. They zoom through there. No, we ought to be providing more facilities for the youngsters, not less.

Fred: Yes, yes. I can see your point.

Shirley: Thing is, what are you going to do? Will you help us?

Fred: Look, I've listened to your arguments. You've a good case and I'm sure there's something I can do.

Shirley: Thanks.

Fred: I'm not promising, mind. But I'll do my best. Now then . . . my round isn't it?

(*He goes off to the bar*)

Shirley: That weren't as difficult as I thought.

Don: I told you he was more reasonable over a pint. Mind you . . . don't be taken in . . . he's a tricky old so and so. But it's a start . . .

13 *A very smart restaurant. Jeremy sits looking at the menu. Fred arrives, out of breath.*

Jeremy: Hello, Fred.

Fred: Hello, Jeremy. Sorry I'm a bit late. Always busy, that's me.

Jeremy: No peace for the wicked, eh?

Fred: Aye.

Jeremy: Here's the menu. The steak's good here, or they do a fine rib of beef.

Fred: Oh aye.

Jeremy: How's it all going? Have the second phase proposals been passed?

Fred: Yes, they've gone through now. But, well, I think we're in for a bit of trouble.

Jeremy: Really? What kind of trouble?

Fred: There's a new councillor. She represents an Action Group in the area, trying to keep the site as a playspace for the kiddies.

Jeremy: Sounds a bit unrealistic, Fred.

Fred: She's got lots of support from the locals. Could be a problem.

Jeremy: Can't they play in the streets? I bet you did as a child.

Fred: You bet I did. Kids today want it cushy.

Jeremy: Seems to me they've just got to realise what a bonus it'll be to have a corporation like mine involved in the area, bringing wealth and prosperity to the borough. Still, if they're worried, I'll see what I can do about landscaping the car park area attached to the block. Perhaps you could consider some point-closures on the roads and then they'll be able to play in safety. That should do it, don't you think?

Fred: Aye. 'Spose so. At least I can tell them I tried and something'll be done.

Jeremy: Yes. Meanwhile, if I were you, I'd get the site fenced off as soon as possible. Avoid trouble. Well, that's that, then. Where you off to for your holiday this year, Fred?

Fred: Holiday? Oh, I haven't thought about it actually.

Jeremy: You know the company has a villa out in Minorca. Nothing grand, but it is let out to the public when the corporation executives aren't using it.

Fred: Sounds nice.

Jeremy: Thing is, if you wanted a couple of weeks out there, I'm sure we could . . . let you have it at an off-season rate.

Fred: Most kind.

Jeremy: Least we can do really. I'm sure the place'd be empty otherwise. Now then, let's eat, shall we? Waiter. . . !

14 *Shirley's home. Shirley is busy sorting through the petition papers and counting the names.*

Jim: Shall we go to the pictures tonight, Shirl?

Shirley: No, Jim, I can't. I've got to attend the Housing Committee meeting.

Jim: What! Not another bloomin' meeting. I don't know Shirley, everything's gone haywire since you started all this politics malarkey.

Shirley: What d'you mean?

Jim: Well, you're never here. You're always out on this committee and that committee. It was one thing organising the play area . . . that was good . . . I quite enjoyed that in the end . . . mucking in and getting it done. But all this, well, it don't seem right.

Shirley: Look Jim, I didn't really want to get involved, you know that. But well . . . something happens and you realise you don't have any power, you don't seem to be able to control your own lives. Unless you *do* something.

Jim: We were doing something. We were building something that people could use. Something for the youngsters like Gary and . . .

Shirley: Yeah, but look what happens. One decision taken by a load of ignorant bores who know nothing, and it's all ruined. Seems to me, people like us ought to make the decisions.

Jim: You've got the power now. What are you doing with it?

Shirley: Oh I don't know, Jim. Sometimes I think you're right, I don't seem to be achieving anything. All the talking and committees and that, and they've still managed to go ahead and fence the whole site in. And I thought I'd got through to Fred Chappell. How do you convince people?

Jim: Umm . . . I s'pose it's like anything else, Shirley, if people don't have first-hand experience of what's going on, they ain't never gonna change. They've got to see for themselves. I mean, what does he know about what it's like to live round here? He's all right, thank you very much, in his little detached number up on that posh housing estate.

Shirley: You're right, you know, Jim. You're dead right.

Jim: Hello, what's going on in your little brain now?

Shirley: An idea. Just an idea. . . .

15 *The street by the Waste.*

Fred: So, this is the famous Waste.

Shirley: It was.

Fred: I can see you did a lot of work. Nice bit of garden . . . play area for kids.

Shirley: Yes.

Fred: You can't say I didn't come and see for myself, can you?

Shirley: Oh yes, you've seen the site, but what about the rest of the neighbourhood, eh? Come on, let me show you round. See how the people live in *your* borough. See the conditions. . . . Come on.

Fred: I knew it.

Shirley: Come and see! (*She walks off*)

Fred: (*Following her*) All right. All right.

Mrs Grant: (*Calling*) Hello, Shirley.

Shirley: Hello, Mrs Grant. How are you, then?

Mrs Grant: Not so bad thanks, considering.

Shirley: Yes, I know. Oh well, bye for now.

Mrs Grant: Bye then.

Shirley: Poor old dear. Has to walk down the stairs in her block, 'cos the lifts are never working. And then waits hours for the bus. Oh you wouldn't know, having a car and all that.

Fred: I know as well as anybody the problems with our public transport.

Shirley: The state of these homes. We need new houses built here, not a flippin' office block.

Fred: You don't have to talk to me as if I didn't know about these conditions. I was brought up in homes like this up North. Didn't do me any harm. Happiest days of my life. You know, the development will bring prosperity to this area.

Shirley: Prosperity? Who for? Not this lot. Not the people who live here. They'll be pushed out, 'cos they won't be able to afford it.

(*Fred is silent as they walk on*)

Shirley: Ah – look. Here's where the kids have to play most of the time. The famous Bensall Crescent.

(*A group of kids are playing football*)

Fred: Football in the street. . . .

Terry: Hi, Shirley.

Shirley: Hello, Terry. Hi John, you be careful now.

Fred: Takes me back. I used to play, just like them.

Shirley: Yeah, but this ain't the thirties with no traffic. Kids need facilities.

Fred: Rubbish. My happiest days were kicking a football around like this. Wall-passes off the kerb. (*Calling*) Hey, come on, give us a kick. Never too old, eh, Shirley?

Shirley: Oh no, be careful, Fred.

Fred: Don't be daft, lass. I haven't forgotten how to kick a ball.

Terry: Here y'are, mister.

(*They pass the ball to Fred. He dribbles it*)

Fred: Now then look at that. Beats one man, beats two . . .

(*The kids notice a car coming*)

Terry: Look out, mister. Car coming.

Fred: I haven't lost the touch. I'll just nod it in the back of the net. . . .

All: Look, mister! Hey, the car!

(*They all turn in horror as the car heads towards Fred. At the last minute he turns and notices, but it is too late. He's knocked over.*)

Shirley: Oh no! Fred, are you all right?

Driver: What did he do that for? The idiot. He was right in the middle of the road. I didn't have a chance to avoid him.

Shirley: Fred, are you OK?

Fred: Yes, I'm all right, I think. It just caught me legs. (*To the driver*) You were driving a bit fast, lad. You realise I'm Councillor Chappell?

Driver: I don't care who you are, you should have more sense, a grown man like you. Playing football in the street. They have playgrounds and parks for that sort of thing you know.

Shirley: Not round here they don't.

Driver: Sorry guv'nor. I hope you've learnt your lesson, that's all.

16 *Outside the Town Hall. The Action Group members are demonstrating as the councillors arrive and go into the Town Hall. They carry placards and chant.*

Crowd: Craig Road for the people, not for the developers! Playgrounds not offices. Support the petition.

(*Shirley arrives*)

Crowd: Good old Shirl. You tell 'em. . . .

Shirley: Great support. You can watch if you like, y'know. The visitors' gallery. You'll have to be quiet, though.

Crowd: OK, Shirley. We're with you.

17 *The Council Chamber.*

Chairperson: And so we come to item 16 on the Agenda – the development plans for the Craig Road site. These are now up for the final 'go-ahead' approval. However, I gather this is an issue about which many local people feel strongly. I have received a petition of several thousand signatures opposing the planned development. I gather Councillor Hayes has a few words.

Shirley: Yes. Look, I won't bore the Council by going over our objections in detail again. All I will say is that in the past, people have questioned just how representative of the community my views are. I think the petition and the massive support here this evening demonstrates the feeling in the neighbourhood. This council has a responsibility to the borough. . . . and the borough isn't just a mass of roads or buildings or schools: it's the people. And the people must decide. I therefore move that the least that can be done at this stage is that the plans be held in abeyance subject to a public enquiry. Let the public choose.

Crowd: Hooray. Right on, Shirley! Well done, Shirl! That's telling 'em.

Chairperson: (*Banging the table*) Quiet please. I must remind you that visitors must remain silent. Now then Councillor Chappell, you've always been an advocate of the scheme to build on this site, would you like to give an alternative view. . . ?

Fred: I must confess I am in something of a dilemma. I still believe the development to be desirable and the best thing for the borough. Yet, I have to concede that the young people in the area certainly need more facilities. I suspect a public enquiry might therefore be the best idea.

Crowd: Hooray. At last he's talking sense. Great! (etc.)

Chairperson: Order, order. . . .

Notes

After a general introduction, specific follow-up notes for each play begin on page 88.

Reading, performance and staging

You can work on these plays in many ways. They can be used for silent reading, or read around the class, but they are best read or performed in small groups. If the class doesn't divide neatly, assign 'directors' to each group.

The director's job is to listen to the read-through and make helpful comments, along the lines of 'This is how it came over to me . . . ' . It's usually best if a director asks questions rather than making negative criticism. 'I wonder if your character is as bossy as that . . ?' 'Perhaps this character should walk away from the situation at that point?' The director may also suggest trying out a new approach. 'What about letting the two characters really lose their temper with each other. . . ?' To begin with, school students will find this difficult, and will need help to avoid an argumentative approach. It's worth persevering with, because as groups become used to discussion they will be developing a language of criticism for themselves.

A further development is to act out the plays in front of the class. Encourage the groups not to become bogged down in detail, and to make do with a simple setting of desks or tables. Two chairs can signify a door or entrance. Very simple or token 'hand-props' (cup and saucer, bag, book or whatever) are useful both to create a character and because they help to avoid the self-consciousness that comes from 'awkward' hands.

Working out moves can be a stumbling-block for inexperienced groups. It's best to forget about memories of Down Left, Up Centre and all the other paraphernalia of proscenium theatre. Go for a logical, motivated approach. If a character enters, ask whether it is from outdoors, or from another room in the same building. If a character goes out, what clues does the script offer about whether it is from the building or into another room?

As you begin to answer these questions, you will find you can plan out a realistic setting. Decide where doors would be, and tables and chairs or any other items that are required for the play's action.

Because the plays were originally written for radio, they each contain several scenes, and it's important to move quickly and fluidly from one to the other. The best way is to put each setting in a different part of the classroom. The remainder of the class – the 'audience' – can sit as they wish in the spaces that are left. ('Promenade' performances such as the National Theatre's medieval productions are a useful model to bear in mind.) An advantage of this kind of staging is its informality. It is much more 'user-friendly' for students who, after all, are not intending to be actors, but simply need drama as a way of articulating issues.

The next step is to work out simple moves. The first ('blocking') rehearsal will have as its purpose sorting out who enters where, who sits or gets up, and at what point in the script. Some moves will become clear, because the script demands them. All of these moves are to make the action believable.

Sometimes groups may wish to take the next step, which is to modify the basic moves so that the stage picture expresses the relationship between characters. This is not as difficult as it sounds, particularly if classes are familiar with creating 'still photographs'. This dramatic convention is very simple. At any point in a play, you can ask the group to devise a 'still picture' which shows what the characters are feeling towards each other. The groups should decide which characters are close to each other and which are distant, which are turned to the other and which are turned away. You can go on to explore more sophisticated metaphors for relationships. 'I feel tugged towards her', 'I can't get far enough away from her' or 'I feel aggressive towards him' can all be given literal expression.

Each group should decide which are the important moments in the play, and devise 'still photos' for them all.

Stage moves then become a matter of moving from one still photo to another, but in a motivated, not a mechanical way.

It is then only a short step to creating a polished performance. At this stage, groups might introduce simple costume, actual props, and in a drama studio, use simple scenery and lights. Where scenery is too difficult (and this is often the case) explore the possibility of working in-the-round, with an audience on all four sides.

In-the-round is rather like radio in not needing scenery, but like radio it needs sound backgrounds. You can record your own, for the 'Waste' in *What Are We Voting For?* or for the distant football chants in *Accident Report*.

Alternatively, you can get commercial records for the mock battle and motorway bypass of *In the Firing Line*. You might explore the possibility of eerie electronic sound to create mood and atmosphere for the strange voices in *Siege at Kangaroo Hill*.

Please note that if you then wish to charge admission to your production, you must first obtain written permission from the publisher on behalf of the writers. This is because, in order to earn a living, they own the performing rights in their plays. This is the way the copyright law works and it applies to you too, if you write a play.

Notes on the plays

In the Firing Line

Discussion and debate

1   Do you agree that the army needs peacetime training grounds?

2   Should land that was taken over during the last war be given back to local Councils?

3   Because of new kinds of weapons, the armed forces may need to take over more land. What conditions should they agree to before doing this?

4   How do you reconcile the military need for training ranges with people's desires that such places should be on other people's land, not their own? What sort of compensation might help people who live next to ranges?

5   What is the connection between Mitchell and Trevor's fight and the main plot?

6   Is it part of human nature to defend home territory?

7   Is there any difference between defending your home territory with fists and with modern weapons?

8   With chairperson, proposers and opposers, debate the motion 'This house considers that pacifism is the only sensible stance in a nuclear world.' Let speakers from the floor join in, and take a vote at the end.

Ideas for writing

1   As Nicola or Trevor, write up an account of the events in the play.

2   Write a description of Lapping Common on Midsummers' Day a hundred years ago.

3   Imagine yourself as a person from a hundred years ago describing Lapping Common as it appears at the time of this play.

4   Imagine that within the next few months, all the roads near where you live are blocked up, houses are emptied, and a training area is established. Either write about the effect this has on a number of characters based on real people you know, or write a realistic adventure story in which you and some friends try to make it impossible for the area to be used.

5   Write the thoughts (the 'stream of consciousness') of a soldier training on Lapping Common. As you dig a trench to give yourself cover, you come across the following objects: a brooch, a faded ribbon, a doll and some notepaper with barely legible writing on it. Develop an imaginary explanation for these objects, while the battle continues overhead.

Drama and role-play

1   Invent the conversation between Trevor and Mrs Matheson in the ambulance.

2   As Mrs Matheson (or an old man in a similar situation) tell a friend why you did what you did in the play.

3   Improvise situations in which you defend your own territory or property against someone else. Explore different kinds of defence.

4   Show how you would have handled the situation if you had gone to visit Major Brookes.

5   Role-play an encounter between a soldier guarding Greenham Common, Molesworth, or a similar base, and a protester who wants the base closed and the land returned to the local people.

6   Devise group situations to show how pacifists might resist attempts to force them to do something they consider to be violent (e.g. on a personal level, someone might try to use force to get something from the pacifist; on a wider level, the government might require the pacifist to do compulsory military service).
    Develop the work by taking one of the situations, and letting two groups of opponents (rather than individuals) become involved. How does passive resistance change when groups are involved?

Siege at Kangaroo Hill

Discussion and debate

1 Summarise what you think are the differences in attitude to land between white Australians and Aboriginal people. (You may need to do some research into 'the Dreaming'.)

2 What do you think are the rights and wrongs of the conflict between Tommy Winmati and his people, and the mining company? How would you try to resolve the conflict?

3 The mining company (and others like it) would not exist if we did not want to buy its products. As Harry Best points out, our desire for soft drinks in cans and for aeroplanes (as well as many other things) ensures that the landscape will go on being dug up. What do you think about this state of affairs? Could it ever be changed?

4 Are there groups of people in the United Kingdom who are treated like the Australian Aboriginals? Who is responsible for their treatment, and what can be done to improve things for them?

5 A famous Australian cartoon from about a hundred years ago has two pictures. The first shows Aboriginal people hunting sheep which are roaming wild like kangaroos. The second shows white settlers shooting the Aboriginal hunters.

   The Aboriginal people thought that animals belonged to the land not to people, and that animals might be hunted for food (but not for sport). They could not understand why sheep were any different from kangaroos, from this point of view.

   On the other hand, the white settlers in Australia were outraged that the Aboriginal people were killing sheep, and thus destroying the wealth of the white people.

   Discuss these two views. What are your own views on ownership, and how would you apply them to animals and other property?

6   Think of as many situations as you can where people's requirements for material goods conflict with other people's social or spiritual needs.

7   Discuss the parallel that Tommy draws between the Aboriginal landscape and churches (or other Western religious buildings and shrines).

Are there parts of our landscape which we have turned into shrines? Are there other landscapes to which this should happen? How good are European-style civilisations at respecting landscapes – and how can the situation be improved?

8   Discuss any thematic similarities between this play and *In the Firing Line*.

Ideas for writing

1   Find out all you can about the Australian outback.

Write an account of how you go off on your own with a friend into the outback. Try to create a particular mood or atmosphere as the story develops.

2   What is 'Hobson's choice' (and who has it in this play)? Write a scene about a person faced with Hobson's choice in a situation you are familiar with. Act it with your friends.

3   Write a short story about a person who is confronted by a difficult choice, and dreams of many voices, some helpful, some confusing. Make sure you tie up the end of your story – don't leave it in mid-air.

4   As Joe Perry, write a report of the 'Siege at Kangaroo Hill'.

5   As a journalist, write an account of the incident for the company newspaper, *The Kangaroo Miner*. Just as you finish, an editor at Reuters (an important international news agency) rings you up to ask you to write a piece which will be sold to newspapers throughout the world. Bearing this new audience in mind, write a second account.

    Swap both pieces with a partner and when you have read each other's stories, discuss how you made the two different, and why.

    What does this tell you about how you should approach reading newspapers?

Drama and role-play

1   Back in England, as Vanessa or Michael, you are asked to give an account of your involvement with Tommy Winmati to the rest of your class.

2   Act out the meeting of Tommy's Aboriginal clan, where they discuss a course of action against the mining company's proposals.

3   As the passer-by in the park, voice your thoughts about the Aboriginal man you have just encountered. Now voice your own thoughts about Tommy, having read the whole play. How do the two descriptions differ?

    Think up other situations where – to an outsider – a person conforms to a stereotype image, but to someone in the know has a very good reason for behaving in such a way.

Why are people so quick to place others in stereotyped moulds?

4   Improvise what happens after the radio news.

5   Suppose the conflict between Tommy Winmati and the mining company goes to court. With one of you as judge, two of you each as counsel for Tommy and for the company, with others as witnesses, such as a mining engineer, young and old Aboriginal people, investors, etc., and the remainder of the class or group as jury, role-play the court case.

Accident Report

This is a series of flashbacks within the framework of a coroner's court. For the play to move quickly when it is staged, it must be easy for characters to move from the witness box to the flashback locations.

Discussion and debate

1   Who do you think was responsible for the train driver's death?

2   Find out about the possible verdict in a coroner's court. If you were the coroner's jury, what verdict would you bring in?

3   Do you think the young football supporters in the play are hooligans?

4   What are the reactions of the older people to the football fans? Are they justified?

5   What do you think are the dangers of flashing barrier level-crossings? Why do you think the older sort with a crossing-keeper living right by the gates might have been safer? What stops British Rail doing away with all level-crossings?

6   What makes driving a train responsible? Do you think piloting an aircraft is so much more responsible that the higher wages are justified?

Ideas for writing

1 If the driver had written a last letter, what might he have said in it?

2 Choose one of the characters, and imagine that you are unable to attend court. You write a statement to be read out on your behalf, in which you state the facts of the accident as your character remembers them.

3 As a journalist, write up the events of this play in such a way as to make them a 'scoop', worthy of front-page headlines.

4 As a Public Relations Officer for British Rail, prepare a press release about the incident.

5 As the coroner, write a balanced report of the events of the play.

6 Write a letter to the *Norton and Cattleford Gazette*, with some ideas for avoiding similar incidents in the future.

Drama and role-play

1 Improvise some of the events of the play, exaggerating them to show clearly how they appeared from the viewpoint of one of the people involved. How likely is it that everyone has a distorted view of the incidents?

2 Improvise a personal situation in which you have 'blown up something out of all proportion'. Present a second, more balanced version.

3 Invent your own incident in which each person has some responsibility for what happens.

What Are We Voting For?

Discussion and debate

1 Do you know of any similar situation which has happened near where you live? Try to remember the issues – what was being developed, what was being pulled down – and the people involved. Were there any

local action groups? What was the outcome?

2   What do you feel about people who come to your door
    to canvass for support? Do you treat them all equally,
    or does the way you respond depend on what they want
    you to do?

3   What are the reasons why the people in the play
    support the Action Group? What other reasons could
    there be? In what circumstances might you support an
    action group?

4   What are the pressures on people like Shirley, who
    take on the running of an action group?

5   Does Jim do enough to support Shirley? What does Jim
    find difficult about the situation? Would it be different
    if their roles were reversed?

6   When the Action Group was first set up, would you
    have voted for Shirley or for Mr Walker? Why?

7   How equal is the struggle between a Council and an
    action group like Shirley's? What – if anything – makes
    it unequal?

8   You may have thought that ordinary people have no
    power to alter things. Has the play helped you to
    change your mind?

9   How much of a say do you have in the running of your
    school? Is there a difference between students voting
    for the way a school is run, and electors voting for a
    councillor? If so, what is the difference?

Ideas for writing

1   As Shirley, write up your diary after some of the
    crucial events in the play. Don't forget to include what
    has been happening at home as well.

2   In groups, 'cast' yourselves as people in the play. Write
    the story of what has happened from the point of view
    of your character. Afterwards, pass your stories around
    the group and talk about how they differ – and why!

3   As reporters, write headlines and articles for the local
    newspaper about the following occasions:
    (a) The formation of the Action Group.

(b) The day the restored Waste is opened to the public.

(c) Mr Perkins' visit.

(d) The local elections for ward councillors.

(e) Fred Chappell's meeting with the developer. (You have had a tip-off from the waiter who overheard everything!)

(f) The protest outside the Council meeting.

Type up your articles as though they are newspaper cuttings, and arrange them in a display.

4   Imagine yourself as a local historian. Write an article about the events in the play for publication in the magazine of the local History Society. Try to weigh up the arguments on both sides to give a balanced view.

5   Write a story of what happens to Jim and Shirley in the future.

6   Write a story about a similar event happening in the town where you live. Choose whether to write the story 'from the outside', or whether to cast yourself as one of the people involved. If you choose the latter, make sure it will become clear to your readers what your involvement is.

Drama and role-play

1   Imagine yourself as Jim, talking to a friend in your 'local'. How does Jim describe what is going on, and his feelings about it on these three occasions?

(a) When Shirley gets elected chairperson of the Action Group.

(b) After a day turning the Waste into a pleasant and relaxing area.

(c) After Shirley has been a councillor for three months.

2   Imagine that, unknown to Councillor Chappell and Jeremy, Shirley is sitting at a nearby table and overhears all! What happens? (There may be better courses of action than simply to confront the two of them.)

3   Role-play doorstep meetings when canvassers ask you

to do something for them. You should not plan in advance what is to happen, and canvassers should decide by themselves what they want to achieve. Householders should decide in advance the sort of person they are, and what causes they might and might not support.

Try canvassing when a householder (a) is very easily persuaded, (b) can be persuaded by good ideas well presented, and (c) only rarely changes their mind. The canvasser should not know in advance which role the householder will take on.

What different technique do canvassers learn?

4 Set up a public meeting where Shirley tries to bring all the issues out into the open. Who would she invite to speak? Will Shirley chair the meeting, or would an independent person be better? If the latter, Shirley can then be a speaker, putting her own points.

Speakers should make notes beforehand. 'Members of the public' should work out their character's history beforehand, so that they can take a realistic part in the meeting.

At the end, a resolution might be put to the meeting by one of the speakers and voted on.

5 In groups, decide on a joint task (e.g. planning a party, or an outing, or a job to be done). As though for real, plan all the stages necessary to get the task done.

When you think you have got everything sorted out, each group member should write down what they think they themselves are supposed to do.

Read out what you have written to the group.

When you have heard everyone, ask yourselves whether on this evidence you could trust your group actually to get the task done!

Finally, ask yourselves how positive each of you were in approaching the planning (or how negative!); whether you were argumentative or tried to sort out differences; how well the group planned all the stages of getting the task done (e.g. who would book seats, who would get the food and drink, who would send out invitations). On reflection, were there important jobs

left out? Is it clear who was to do what, or will
vagueness lead to some things being done twice and
other important things not being done at all?

What does this role-play tell you about how groups
operate? What lessons have you learnt for the next
time you're a member of a group with a job to do?

The Save Our School Simulation

This is a role-play simulation in the form of an Inquiry. Its
purpose is to give classes an insight into the social forces
involved in balancing between town development and
conservation. At the same time, it is a useful teaching aid
for encouraging students to express themselves on issues
well within their grasp, as well as providing an opportunity
to discuss how local democracy works.

The class is split into groups of two or three and each
group is given one of the role-cards. If time is short, some
of the roles may be combined. Each role is printed below,
and may be photocopied and stuck on card. Role-players
must be given time to assimilate the brief on their
role-card.

The teacher or a responsible member of the class is
appointed Inspector. The simulation is allowed to run its
course under their control. Each role is called upon to
speak, using the notes on the role-card as a basis. It is the
job of the person or group in each role to 'sell' their point
of view as strongly as they can (which will require them to
elaborate on the 'bare bones' provided). After each
role-player has spoken, they may be questioned by the rest
of the group.

It is important to create an appropriate sense of
formality. This can be done partly by rearranging classroom
furniture into a suitable layout for an inquiry. The teacher
can set an example by insisting on correct forms of address
such as, 'I now call upon (name of student), Broom Leigh
Town Planning Officer. . . '.

When all the roles have spoken, the teacher asks
everyone to imagine themselves in the Inspector's role and
to discuss what recommendations they would make.

It is up to the teacher or chairman to decide when the

simulation can go no further. At this point the class should be invited to come out of role and to discuss what they have learnt. This 'debriefing' is often as important as the simulation itself.

The roles are these:

the Inspector, who acts as chairperson
the property developer
the developer's architect
a member of Broom Leigh Chamber of Commerce
the chairperson of the Council Planning Committee
the Senior Planning Officer
the leader of the Council opposition
the chairperson of the Save Our School campaign
the chairperson of Broom Leigh Residents' Association
a spokesperson for Broom Leigh Heritage

Each of these can be role-played as a small group rather than as an individual. If time is short, combine these roles: property developer and developer's architect; Planning Committee Chairperson and Planning Officer; Residents' Association and Broom Leigh Heritage.

The sense of reality can be heightened by inventing a map of Broom Leigh, showing the High Street, Parish School, Regent's Gardens and the outline of the Mall development. Invent names, and buildings of historic interest.

CHAIRPERSON (THE INSPECTOR)

Broom Leigh is a rapidly growing town on the edge of a large city. The Council wants to see the town centre renewed at a time when property values are soaring. Unfortunately the old Parish School and its extensive playground stands in the way of any redevelopment, as do the adjoining Regent's Gardens. The Council want to pull the school down, but many local people wish to resist this move.

Because of the resulting deadlock, the matter has gone to Inquiry. This room has been designated the Court of Inquiry, and Her Majesty's Secretary of State has appointed me (or give the name of one of the students) as Inspector. I shall call witnesses in the following order: the developers, the council and objectors. Each witness may be cross-examined by representatives of the other groups. At the end of the Inquiry, I shall consider the evidence and make a recommendation as to the future of the Parish School.

THE PROPERTY DEVELOPER

I have had a long association with Broom Leigh, and my grandfather owned a sweet shop here. He and my grandmother went to school in Broom Leigh.

I am putting forward a plan to develop the town centre. My architect will develop the plan in detail, but the basics of the scheme are these.

Broom Leigh's centre is one long High Street which is always congested with traffic. There are good department stores and traditional shops with frontages along the High Street, and people come from the surrounding villages and suburbs to shop. Yet as things stand the centre is cramped and out of date. There is no room for further growth, and shopping for most people is an unpleasant experience of queuing for space in a car park, only to be elbowed and jostled when you finally get into the shops. Simply put, Broom Leigh has to expand, and the only question is where the expansion can take place.

The Parish School site and Regent's Gardens are the only open spaces which can be considered for development. They are just behind the High Street and offer a sufficient area to enable my company to build an elegant and spacious shopping Mall. There would be room for a high-rise carpark and access road which would serve the needs of the community for the foreseeable future.

THE DEVELOPER'S ARCHITECT

We plan a large and sensitive development. The shopping mall will have space for over 100 new shopping units. Some will be very large, for supermarkets and department stores, while the smaller units will be available for traditional retail outlets such as specialist food shops, bookshops and chemists.

The Mall will have an exciting steel and glass-roofed construction, combined with traditional cladding materials such as brick and tiles. From a distance the development will be a symbol to those approaching Broom Leigh of its new-found style and attractiveness. The Mall will ensure that Broom Leigh continues to be a commercial focus of the surrounding community for many years to come.

Inside the Mall there will be a central relaxation area with seating, pools and fountains, and the opportunity to create a conservatory garden with a combination of low-level borders and tall screening plants. Radiating from the relaxation area will be shopping ways with escalators to the first floor. The public will enjoy shopping in pleasant all-weather surroundings, a far cry from old-fashioned High Street fumes and congestion.

At the rear of the Mall, lifts will take shoppers to a large carpark with easy access to Broom Leigh ring road. Truly, the Mall will make shopping a new experience.

A MEMBER OF BROOM LEIGH CHAMBER OF COMMERCE

My members support the Mall wholeheartedly and enthusiastically. The old town centre needs a new injection of life. That means room for business expansion. Most of my members have to carry out their business and their trading from cramped, inadequate and old-fashioned premises. The Mall will change all this.

Moreover, the Mall will act as a dynamo for new private enterprise. Businesses will flock to Broom Leigh, marking a new era of prosperity. And of course, in the wake of these new businesses will come new employment opportunities. As it is, unemployment in the area is far too high. We would be fools to let this opportunity pass us by.

THE SENIOR PLANNING OFFICER

The centre of Broom Leigh was designated an area of trade and commerce as long ago as 1974. Even then, it was recognised that the old Parish School was an intrusion into the designated area. Furthermore, when the dual carriageway, Broom Leigh Relief Road, was built in 1985 with the object of relieving High Street congestion, sections of it had to remain as single carriageway because of protests from parents at the Parish School.

The present owners of the school are the Council. Council plan to demolish the school in order to complete the four-laning of the Relief Road, and – what is more important – to provide an adequate land area for the Mall. We have been unable to find any developer prepared to create a shopping mall unless the Parish School site and Regent's Gardens become available. Without them, the remaining land area is too small to develop.

THE CHAIRPERSON OF THE COUNCIL PLANNING COMMITTEE

In outline and subject to negotiation of detail, my committee is poised to recommend acceptance of the plan. Broom Leigh town centre is in urgent need of renewal. The new Mall is a sensitive use of the area which is shortly to become available.

Moreover, the income of the Council from the new shopping units will far exceed the income from the present hotchpotch of shops along the High Street. When the Mall is fully operational, we shall see a net increase of 15 per cent in the Council's revenue. The upshot of this will be no rise in either rates or poll-tax for the foreseeable future.

THE LEADER OF THE COUNCIL OPPOSITION

When I went to the Parish School in 1937, Broom Leigh was a small market town with a character all of its own. Over the years, the developers have moved in, and we are in danger of seeing our beautiful town become another Croydon, or Milton Keynes or Cumbernauld.

My party does not stand for putting the clock back. We recognise that all communities have to evolve and develop – without change, communities stagnate, unemployment rises and the young and enterprising drift away.

We want to see new development, but development on a human scale. We don't want ugly, impersonal new buildings. We want to retain the character of the old and at the same time encourage good new approaches. The Mall may have a very pleasant relaxation area in the centre, but what will the multi-storey car park look like outside? We are told that income from the shopping units will be so high that local rates and taxes can be kept down. That money won't come from nowhere – it will come from higher prices in the new shops!

The same will happen in Broom Leigh as elsewhere – little one-man businesses and shops which give our town its character will be forced out. In their place will be yet more chain-stores. Broom Leigh will be no different from other newly-developed towns up and down the country.

I, and all the Councillors who vote with me, say 'Reject this scheme!' Let us evolve and develop, but on a human scale. The best of the new with the best of the old!

THE CHAIRPERSON OF THE SAVE OUR SCHOOL
CAMPAIGN

The Parish School has existed on its present site for nearly two
hundred years. It began as a little school with local people paying a
penny a week for their children to attend. Later it became the
Parish School attached to the Parish church. In 1875 it was taken
over by the local authority as a Voluntary Aided School. So for
many years, the Parish School has been a focus for our community.

Many famous local people passed through its gates, including
three mayors of Broom Leigh, two chairmen of the Chamber of
Commerce, as well as the famous novelist J.D. Banks, and the
nuclear physicist John Pennyweather.

Today, the school is as successful as ever it was. Pupils gain
inspiration from the famous men and women who have gone before
them. The school is part of Broom Leigh's heritage, and to knock it
down would be an act of vandalism.

THE CHAIRPERSON OF BROOM LEIGH RESIDENTS' ASSOCIATION

Broom Leigh Residents' Association is firmly against any development of Broom Leigh centre on the contemplated scale. We have enough department stores already, and they are big enough for the needs of people here.

The real problem is that the stores and the council are hand-in-glove to attract more and more custom, without for one moment stopping to think what the increase in trade does to the town. Do they ever try to shop in the crowded town centre, full of people from many miles around? Only last Saturday someone stopped me to ask the way to the High Street. They had come to shop from twenty miles away! And as for congestion, that's terrible – it can take twenty minutes to get through the High Street during the day. Parking is just as bad. Most residents leave their cars at home.

The shopping mall won't solve any of these problems. It may alleviate them for a few months, until advertising spreads the word, and then even more people will come from further afield still! All the present problems will come back again, but on a much larger scale. It'll be endless!

The real problem is with our Council. They are money-grubbers. They don't care about the environment or the town centre, so long as they can keep the local rates and taxes down! They certainly don't care about people.

We say that any local development should be small-scale and in keeping with the current appearance of the town.

SPOKESPERSON FOR BROOM LEIGH HERITAGE

There is much of historical note about Broom Leigh. It was a market town and a staging post on the stagecoach route from the city to the coast. It has a Market Cross dating from medieval times, and the Parish Church incorporates part of the original Anglo-Saxon nave.

There are many fine buildings dating back to the eighteenth and nineteenth centuries – evidence of a long and prosperous past.

The Parish School is an important historical link with the past, and part of the town's heritage. Its playing field and the adjoining Regent's Gardens are surrounded by large and beautiful hardwood trees, mainly oaks and chestnuts. Both spaces together form a lung, or green area very close to the centre of town. They are a reminder of Broom Leigh's past as a country market town, as well as a very necessary recreation space for local people and shoppers alike.

The shopping mall, if it were built, would destroy no less than ten buildings of historic interest, as well as many mature trees surrounding the Parish School playing field and Regent's Gardens. The school itself would be an unforgivable loss.

The scheme envisaged by the developers is a desecration. The Council will become little better that vandals. Indeed there is only one difference between the Council and vandals – damage by vandals can be repaired, but the destruction now being contemplated by the Council can never be restored.